INDIE AUTHOR MAGAZINE

HELLO AND WELCOME!

I'm Indie Annie, and I'm thrilled you're reading this gorgeous full-color version of IAM. Did you know that you can also access all the information, education, and inspiration in our app? It's available on both the iOS App Store and Google Play. And for those that prefer to listen to me read articles, you can pop over to Spotify or our website.

Happy Reading!

IndieAuthorMagazin

I0106252

Download on the **App Store**

GET IT ON **Google Play**

Spotify

The Self Publishing Show LIVE!

THE SOUTHBANK CENTRE, LONDON
25TH & 26TH JUNE 2024

Once again sponsored by Amazon KDP and attended by hundreds of authors plus major industry players including: Audible, Reedsy and ProWritingAid, Europe's premier indie author conference is going to be bigger and better than ever.
The 2024's two day line up features the amazing EL James, Lucy Score, Steve Higgs, Sacha Black, Craig Martelle, Rachel McLean and many more.

TICKETS AVAILABLE NOW: learnselfpublishing.com/spslive

SPS Live 2024
SCHEDULE

kindle direct publishing

DAY 1 – TUESDAY 25TH JUNE 2024

9.00 AM	WELCOME · JAMES BLATCH
9.10 AM	YOU CAN TOO! · STEVE HIGGS
9.45 AM	THE THREE SECRETS OF FINDING YOUR AUDIENCE · SUZY K QUINN
10.30 AM	BREAK
11.00 AM	3 STRATEGIES TO PROMOTE NEW RELEASES WITH BOOKBUB ADS · AUDREY DEROBERT
11.35 AM	AI: FEAR, LOATHING & ACCEPTANCE · JAMES BLATCH
12.10 PM	LSP COURSES UPDATE · RICARDO FAYET & JAMES BLATCH
12.30 PM	LUNCH
1.30 PM	CRACKING THE AUDIOBOOK CODE · CRAIG THOMSON
2.15 PM	HOOKING ONE MILLION READERS · E.L. JAMES & LUCY SCORE
3.00 PM	BREAK
3.30 PM	THE FUTURE OF AUDIO BOOKS PANEL · RACHEL MCLEAN, MILES STEVENS-HOARE FROM WF HOWES, VICTORIA GERKEN FROM PODIUM AUDIO & WILL DAGES FROM FINDAWAY VOICES BY SPOTIFY
4.35 PM	GENERATIVE AI & EDITING · HAYLEY MILLIMAN
5.15 PM	FINISH

DAY 2 – WEDNESDAY 26TH JUNE 2024

9.00 AM	DAY 2 INTRODUCTION · JAMES BLATCH
9.05 AM	WORDS HAVE VALUE: MAKING THE LEAP TO BECOMING A FULL-TIME AUTHOR WITH KDP · HANNH LYNN, CLARE LYDON AND SACHA BLACK
9.50 AM	FINDING HUNGRY READERS · ALEX NEWTON
10.25 AM	EFFECTIVELY USING EMAIL PROMOS: FROM INBOX TO BESTSELLER · MIKE HOURIGAN
11.00 AM	BREAK
11.30 AM	DEEP DIVE INTO AUDIBLE · LEE JARIT
12.05 PM	UNLOCKING THE POTENTIAL OF YOUR AUTHOR WEBSITE · STUART GRANT
12.45 PM	THE NEXT STEP IN YOUR AUTHOR CAREER · RACHEL MCLEAN
1.30 PM	LUNCH
2.30 PM	WIDEN YOUR WORLD · DAN WOOD
3.05 PM	THE DIRECT SELLING ECOSYSTEM · DAMON COURTNEY
3.50 PM	DEALING WITH CHANGE · CRAIG MARTELLE
4.20 PM	GOODBYE · JAMES BLATCH
4.40 PM	FINISH

Please note:
Conference sessions are subject to change at short notice.

LONDON

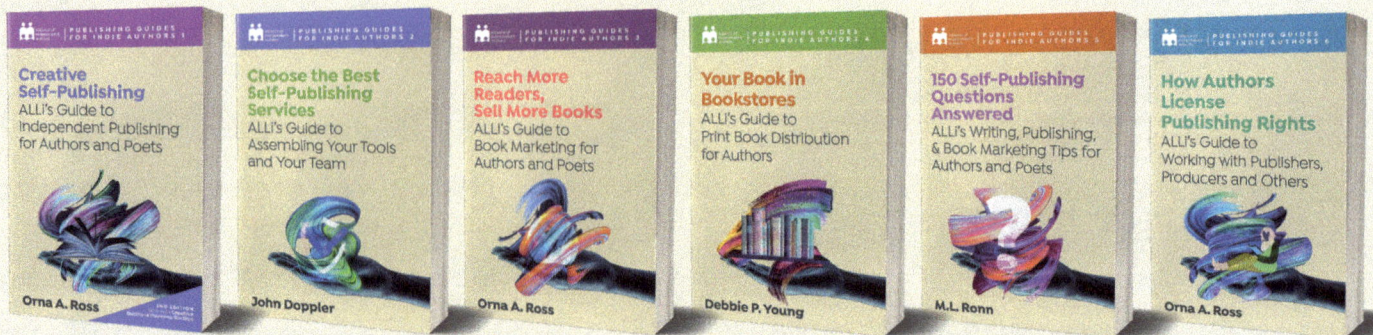

"I joined while having a crisis with Amazon KDP... The Alliance is a beacon of light. I recommend that all indie authors join...
Susan Marshall

"The Alliance is about standing together.
Joanna Penn

"It's the good stuff, all on one place.
Richard Wright

"ALLi has helped me in myriad ways: discounts on services, vetting providers, charting a course to sales success. But more than anything it's a community of friendly, knowledgeable, helpful people."
Beth Duke

See hundreds more testimonials at:
AllianceIndependentAuthors.org/testimonials

MARKET RESEARCH

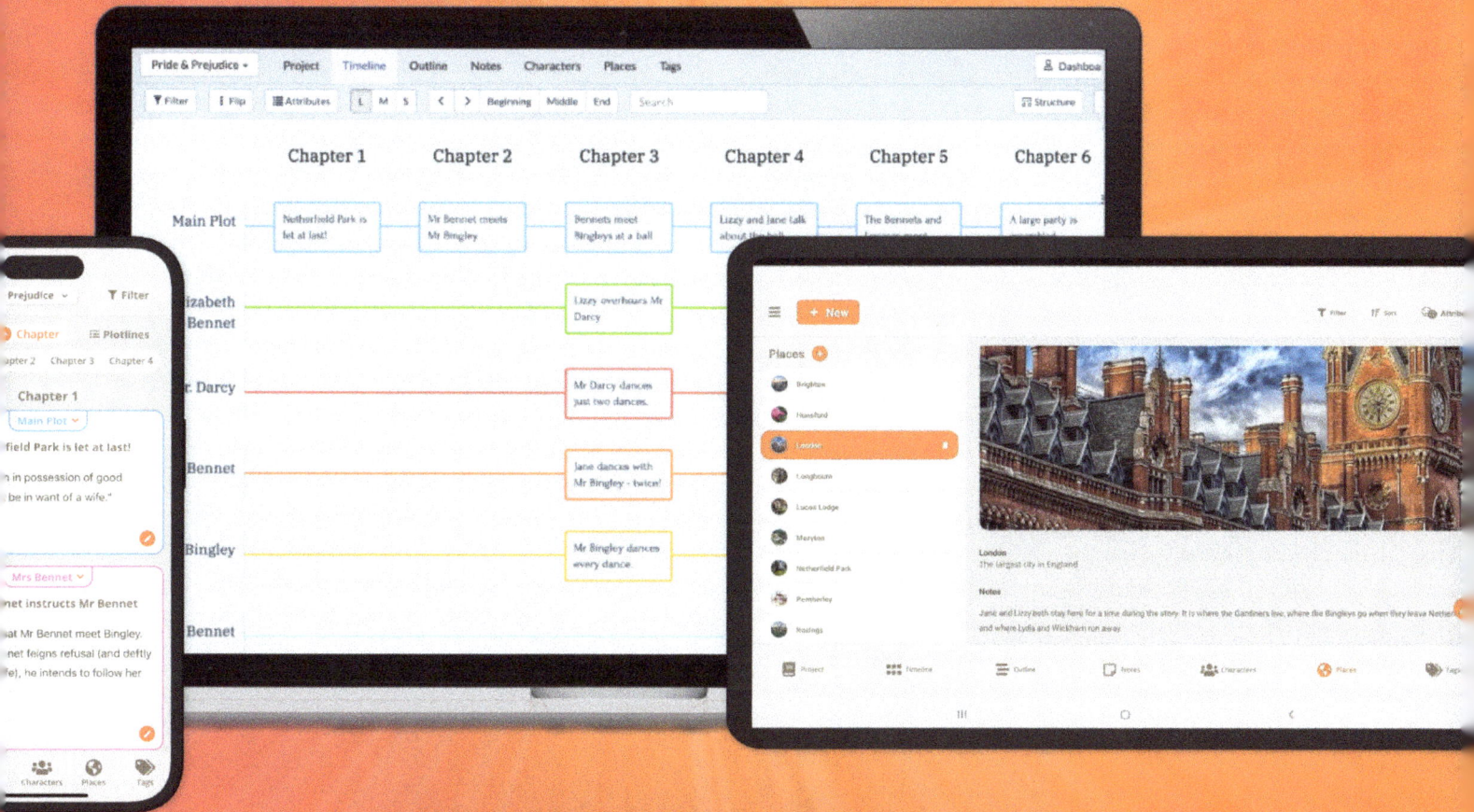

Authorpreneurs in Action

"I love Lulu! They've been a fantastic distributor of my paperbacks and an excellent partner as I dive into direct sales. They integrate so smoothly with my personal Shopify store, and their customer support has been top notch."

Katie Cross, katiecrossbooks.com

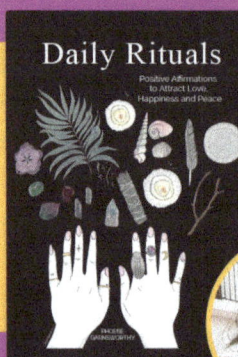

"Having my own store has given me the freedom to look at my creativity as a profitable business and lifelong career."

Phoebe Garnsworthy, phoebegarnsworthy.com

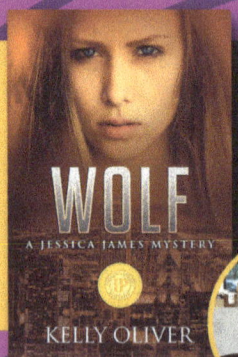

"Lulu has a super handy integration with Shopify. Lulu makes it so easy to sell paperbacks directly to readers."

Kelly Oliver, kellyoliverbooks.com

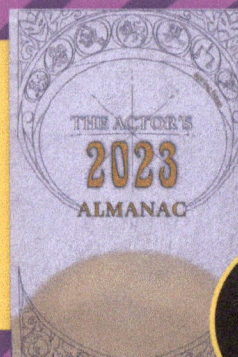

"My experience with Lulu Direct has been more convenient and simple than I anticipated or thought possible. I simply publish, take a step back and allow the well-oiled machine to run itself. Most grateful!"

Molly McGivern, theactorsalmanac.com

INDIE
AUTHOR MAGAZINE

EDITORIAL

Publisher | Chelle Honiker

Editor in Chief | Nicole Schroeder

Creative Director | Alice Briggs

ADVERTISING & MARKETING

Inquiries
Ads@AtheniaCreative.com

Information
https://IndieAuthorMagazine.com/
advertising/

CONTRIBUTORS

Angela Archer, Elaine Bateman, Patricia Carr, Bradley Charbonneau, Honorée Corder, Jackie Dana, Heather Clement Davis, Jamie Davis, Laurel Decher, Fatima Fayez, Gill Fernley, Greg Fishbone, Jen B. Green, Jac Harmon, Marion Hermannsen, Steve Higgs, Chrishaun Keller-Hanna, Kasia Lasinska, Monica Leonelle, Jenn Lessmann, Megan Linski-Fox, Craig Martelle, Angie Martin, Merri Maywether, Kevin McLaughlin, Lasairiona McMaster, Jenn Mitchell, Tanya Nellestein, Russell Nohelty, Susan Odev, Eryka Parker, Tiffany Robinson, Clare Sager, Joe Solari, Becca Syme, David Viergutz

SUBSCRIPTIONS
https://indieauthormagazine.com/subscribe/

HOW TO READ
https://indieauthormagazine.com/how-to-read/

WHEN WRITING MEANS BUSINESS
IndieAuthorMagazine.com

Athenia Creative | 6820 Apus Dr., Sparks, NV, 89436 USA | 775.298.1925

ISSN 2768-7880 (online)–ISSN 2768-7872 (print)

THE NEW WAY FOR READERS TO FIND AUTHORS SELLING DIRECT

DIRECT2READERS

A unique directory where you can connect directly with your fans and keep all your hard-earned profits.

💡 Innovative Recommendation Engine: Our natural language recommendation engine helps readers discover books based on their preferences. Say goodbye to clunky categories!

📈 New Market Access: Gain exposure to a new segment of avid readers, all hungry for fresh indie voices.

💵 Zero Commissions: You read it right! We don't take a cut. Your profits are yours to keep.

🚀 Boost Your Sales: Benefit from our advanced marketing and influencer channels designed to supercharge your direct sales.

🌐 **Register Now**
Direct2Readers.com

From the EDITOR IN CHIEF

I've never considered myself much of a sports fan, but the Olympics have always been an easy exception to make. I remember waking up early to watch cycling during the Rio Olympic Games in 2016 and setting reminders on my phone for gymnastics events held at the Tokyo Games in 2021. It's a safe bet my writing soundtrack will shift from movie scores to sports announcements over the next couple of weeks.

But there's more that we, as authors, can take from the games than just entertainment. Although writing sprints may not quite have made it to the Olympic stage yet—though they certainly should—as *IAM* staff writer Laurel Decher points out in this month's issue, the Olympics can offer us important lessons on understanding our audiences and growing our author businesses.

Part of marketing is understanding your ideal reader and the things that they want to see; there's a reason Olympics organizers have added new sports in recent years to reflect the interests of younger generations, like this year's breaking, sport climbing, skateboarding, and surfing will do. For us authors, that's where market research and creating a reader avatar can come into play. Catering to your ideal reader doesn't mean you're excluding fans. Being a horseback rider, I've always watched equestrian three-day eventing, but I'll also happily tune in to sports I never even known existed as long as they seem interesting. Knowing what your target audience likes simply helps you maintain your focus so that the readers you most want to reach will be satisfied. In some ways, it makes your business decisions easier—and like this month's Mindset article emphasizes, that's always a plus.

Our books don't need to be gold-medal worthy in every reader's eyes, as long as they make your superfans happy. Let the Olympics be an example—if your audience is excited enough that they wake up early to read your book or set reminders on their phones for your new release, you've come out on top.

Nicole Schroeder
Editor in Chief
Indie Author Magazine

Nicole Schroeder is a storyteller at heart. As the editor in chief of Indie Author Magazine, she brings nearly a decade of journalism and editorial experience to the publication, delighting in any opportunity to tell true stories and help others do the same. She holds a bachelor's degree from the Missouri School of Journalism and minors in English and Spanish. Her previous work includes editorial roles at local publications, and she's helped edit and produce numerous fiction and nonfiction books, including a Holocaust survivor's memoir, alongside independent publishers. Her own creative writing has been published in national literary magazines. When she's not at her writing desk, Nicole is usually in the saddle, cuddling her guinea pigs, or spending time with family. She loves any excuse to talk about Marvel movies and considers National Novel Writing Month its own holiday.

The Courage to Keep Writing

Everyone is afraid of something. When it comes to your author career, there's the fear that your book won't be well received. That you'll get bad reviews. That your brand will become tainted in some way. Pirates! There are a million things to send you into a dark corner, quaking.

Courage brings you back into the daylight because the rewards can be vast. Like the man in the arena, only you are in there, fighting. It's easy for others to criticize, belittle, or demean when they risk nothing to do it. Complainers and whiners accomplish less, if anything at all.

Doers bear the burdens of a society of watchers. Stand up and be counted! Shout to all with ears to hear, "I'm an author." There will be those who try to beat you down, but they're not in the arena. If they are, they'll only attack you because they fear you. Stand proud of who you are and what you are.

You are an author. You write books. There are many people who say they're going to write a book but never do. It takes courage to put pen to paper and even more courage to publish it for anyone to see. You deserve praise.

You also have to know that it's not your best work, not right away. Writing takes practice. It's you against yourself. Write, and keep writing until you can say it's your best work. Then sit back for a moment and enjoy the feeling. And get back to writing, with the courage of your convictions and the experience to know what's best for your business.

Be the one in the arena, knowing that you're competing no matter how much you may be afraid—whether you admit it.

You can't win if you don't play.

This was my last article for *Indie Author Magazine*. I hope you enjoyed the monthly column and wish you the best for a great future as an author. ∎

Craig Martelle

Craig Martelle

High school Valedictorian enlists in the Marine Corps under a guaranteed tank contract. An inauspicious start that was quickly superseded by excelling in language study. Contract waived, a year at the Defense Language Institute to learn Russian and off to keep my ears on the big red machine during the Soviet years. Earned a four-year degree in two years by majoring in Russian Language. My general staff. career included choice side gigs - UAE, Bahrain, Korea, Russia, and Ukraine.

Major Martelle. I retired from the Marines after a couple years at the embassy in Moscow working arms control issues.

Department of Homeland Security then law school next. I was working for a high-end consulting firm performing business diagnostics, business law, and leadership coaching. For the money they paid me, I was good with that. Just until I wasn't. Then I started writing.

Invest in the Best of Your Business

Should authors "write to market"? It's a question we've answered before, but this month, we're looking at a more practical question: if you want to understand what's going on in the market in which you are doing business, how do you go about it? Where can you find the best facts and figures to help your writing and publishing choices? Many authors seem afraid of "data," yet there is no industry that does not use information to help it make good commercial choices.

The Alliance of Independent Authors (ALLi) commissions original research and compiles facts and figures across the industry, making it one of the best sources of data on self-publishing in the world. You can find multiple readable reports at https://allianceindependentauthors.org/facts, offering insights relevant to indie authors on publishing business trends, such as selling direct, using AI tools for marketing, distribution trends, and craft-related decisions about things like writing diverse characters or writing stand-alones versus series.

Beyond these initial facts and figures, though, let's look at where to find more specific information relevant to every stage of your writing and publishing business.

BEGINNER AUTHORS: INVEST YOUR TIME

Market research can be 100 percent free; what it does take is a bit of your time. Go on Amazon, Kobo, Barnes & Noble, and other retail platforms, and look at your own genre and categories to see what it takes to make stories like yours sell. What do the other books look like? What kinds of cover trends can you spot? Sometimes the font, colors, and suitable visuals are obvious and a real boon for briefing cover designers. How are the blurbs worded? Are there certain buzzwords and tones of voice used?

Look at the editorial reviews and any awards won by other authors; both can indicate reviewers and awards that would be suitable for you to approach. Pay attention to where a distribution site suggests other authors who readers often enjoy, and look at those authors' platforms to understand what you might have in common and how they market themselves.

Check each site's ranked titles as well. Which books are in the Top 100 in the overall store, and which books are still selling well many years after publication?

Then look at the reader reviews. What are readers saying? What aspects of the books are they valuing? What words and phrases do they use that you'd like them to use about your books?

All of this can guide you on your choice of genres or subgenres, covers, and blurbs, and help you decide which reviewers and awards to include in your marketing plans. Read widely in your category too; even just reading online samples will indicate common stylistic options that you can consider when making your own craft choices.

ALLi's "Ultimate Guide to Understanding Your Book Genre for Indie Authors," about getting into the nitty-gritty of your genre, has excellent tips for conducting this kind of research and can be found at https://self-publishingadvice.org/understanding-your-genre.

EMERGING AUTHORS: INVEST IN TOOLS

When it comes to the publishing market, you may not always need to do all the digging yourself. There are valuable market research tools in which authors can invest where someone else has done the legwork for you. Two in particular that are of use and relatively affordable are K-Lytics and Publisher Rocket by Kindlepreneur. K-Lytics offers genre-specific reports—almost forty at last count—that analyze thousands of Amazon books and sales trends to offer information on everything from cover color trends to which subgenre niches are growing or fading away. Check the K-Lytics website at https://k-lytics.com/shop to see if your category is covered.

Publisher Rocket gives authors information on the most searched-for keywords to use in your metadata and category insights such as what percentage of the category comprises traditional or indie authors, the average page count, whether the whole category is growing or declining over time, and more. Learn more about the platform at https://publisherrocket.com. If you're feeling busy, allow these tools to do the heavy lifting for you and enjoy their insights at the click of a button.

EXPERIENCED AUTHORS: INVEST IN YOUR OWN DATA

As well as external market data, as you grow in experience and time spent as an author, the most important consideration is your own

data, which will build up on retail and distribution platforms and via analytics on your own website and any ads platforms you use. Which calls-to-action (CTAs) work best inside your books? Which pages do your website visitors linger on, and which do they bounce away from most quickly? Did your sales go up when you changed your covers?

Take your best reviews and make a word cloud of them to understand what your readers value most in your writing. When you have a wide back catalog, try advertising your overall author brand rather than individual titles or series. To help with this, add up how many five-star reviews you've received across all your books, as a few thousand can be a strong piece of social proof.

Being able to see more of your own data is, of course, something that interests many indie authors about selling books from their own website. It isn't just about the higher profit margins you'll receive but also about the chance to keep and analyze all customer data, leading to greater engagement and better communication with your most loyal readers. ALLi has multiple posts on how direct sales can benefit your business, from e-books to print, and the mindset shift it takes.

- https://selfpublishingadvice.org/selling-books-on-your-author-website
- https://selfpublishingadvice.org/print-books-direct
- https://selfpublishingadvice.org/podcast-direct-sales

If you're considering something like a Kickstarter project, browse several projects in the publishing category and back some projects yourself to see how it all feels. Note what kinds of rewards are being offered, the tone and frequency of communications, the visuals used, and more; all of it will give you important insights into how to set up a successful Kickstarter of your own. Once the campaign is over, always review what went well and what you could do better next time—in writing.

Remember, even if you have a passion project burning in your heart, that doesn't mean you can't also do your research and ensure your marketing plans are built into the book. A December 2023 episode from ALLi's *Publishing for Profit* podcast, "Bake Marketing Into Your Writing Process," explores doing just that.

Finally, a reminder that market research opportunities are everywhere. Don't just look at the publishing industry; also look beyond it to understand the bigger picture. For example, Mintel's annual Global Trends recently identified that consumers want more "experiences" and fewer "things." How might you market your books as an experience rather than a product?

Market research can be a fun activity leading to significant commercial and creative rewards. Enjoy! ∎

Melissa Addey, ALLi Campaigns Manager

Melissa Addey, ALLi Campaigns Manager

The Alliance of Independent Authors (ALLi) is a global membership association for self-publishing authors. A non-profit, our mission is ethics and excellence in self-publishing. Everyone on our team is a working indie author and we offer advice and advocacy for self-publishing authors within the literary, publishing and creative industries around the world. www.allianceindependentauthors.org

Know How to Read Your Readers

In the second installment of his quarterly series, Managing Director of Author Nation and business expert Joe Solari explores what it takes to build your audience as an indie author. Most industry advice focuses on targeting new readers and drawing them into your funnel—but what about the superfans you already have? Solari says the key to growing an authentic readership is fostering the one you already have.

In our last discussion, we explored the tactical elements of launching a book and evaluating its success. Today, we're broadening our perspective to focus on the overarching trends that are reshaping the publishing landscape. As Brad Jacobs, an influential CEO, wisely stated in his book *How to Make a Few Billion Dollars*, "You can make a lot of mistakes and succeed if you get the big trend right." This statement sets the stage for our exploration of the shift from artificial intelligence to general machine intelligence and its potential impact on publishing.

UNDERSTANDING THE BIG PICTURE

Rather than getting lost in the minutiae of innovations and market fluctuations, let's draw lessons from the past. Consider the 1990s' internet boom—nobody could have precisely predicted the dominant platforms and mediums that would emerge. Similarly, the future of publishing is uncertain, but one thing is clear: Focusing on your content and audience is crucial.

This isn't a new idea, but it's often overlooked. Many discussions about discoverability treat it as a commodity to be bought and sold. However, true discovery is more akin to a "meet-cute" with a potential superfan. The key to long-term success is to deliver content authentically, in a way that makes your audience proud to associate with your brand. Often, the driver for adopting a new way to market is that you see someone else succeed. Before jumping in, however, ask yourself these questions:

Does this fit with my brand?

Joe Solari

Joe Solari is an author, entrepreneur, and consultant. Since 2016 he has been helping best-selling authors build great publishing businesses. He has worked to create tools and systems to help passionate business owners professionalize their team and operations to achieve exceptional results.

Will my existing customers love this new thing?

Can I find an entirely new audience who will enjoy my brand doing this new thing?

Every decision and market change should be evaluated against this standard: does it enhance your ability to produce the best content for your audience?

DEEP DIVE INTO AUDIENCE RESEARCH

Most writing advice focuses on identifying your current demographics to target ideal new audiences. I suggest focusing more on what makes your existing fans connect with your brand. You want to learn how to better ignite that brand enthusiasm rather than profile your readers.

Focus inward. Start small to grow big. Instead of casting a wide net with your market research, focus on understanding the real motivations of your current audience. Emotional connection, not price, drives loyalty. Collect first-party and zero-party data—direct feedback and behavioral insights from your audience. Offer ways for readers to get in touch, like surveys or short emails with open-ended questions. Use this data to build customer avatars and better understand what motivates your audience, which can help you attract similar fans.

Build from what you have. Leverage AI tools to enhance your understanding of your ideal reader.

Set up the AI to mimic your readers' preferences and ask it specific questions about what they seek in a reading experience. This approach can yield creative, tailored strategies for engagement.

Explore new markets thoughtfully. When expanding into new markets like direct selling or subscriptions, thoroughly research what these new audiences desire. Understand that they may want something different from what you or your existing audience wants. For example, if you're considering Kickstarter, research whether there is an audience for your content there and how they prefer to engage with projects.

Write to market 2.0: Finally, try to evolve with your audience. Observe how your audience's interests change over time—the shows they watch, the music they listen to—and align your content with these shifting tastes. This improves discoverability and ensures that your content remains relevant and engaging.

By focusing on these strategic elements—big trend awareness, authentic content delivery, and deep audience understanding—you can navigate the complexities of the publishing world more effectively. Let's continue to leverage research and creativity to serve our audiences better. Together, we can adapt and thrive in the ever-changing landscape of publishing. ■

Joe Solari

Dear Indie Annie,

I know it's important to understand who you're writing and marketing to, but how do I develop my ideal reader avatar? Every time I try, it feels like I'm limiting myself.

Needing to Niche Down

Dear Niche,

Oh darling, focusing on your target audience feels as frightening as finalizing a paint palette for your parlor. Why choose when there are so many gorgeous colors to pick from? But defining your ideal reader liberates your creativity to flourish, not flounder! It helps you craft stories and connections tailored to those most eager for your tales.

First, study your current cheer squad for clues. Who are the devoted fans who get your style and have tastes most in tune with your creative vision? What do these existing fans have in common? Age? Interests? Values? Analyze reviews and engage with readers to identify unifying threads. Cater to those taste buds, whether they prefer Mystery, Romance, or more. Build on what devotees are already drooling over. Just like creating a Pinterest board, it's time to get out the virtual swatches and paint charts.

Then get imaginative! Envision the ideal reader drinking in your words in a kitchen designed with them in mind. Create avatars who represent these amazing people. Take copious notes. Build them up as you would characters in your book. Think about their personalities, professions, habits, quirks, and dreams. Make them vivid, not vague: Felicity, the thirty-something bold baker enthralled by Magical Realism. Ivan, the new retiree seeking Adventure stories to inspire global travels. Is Clara your children's book avatar, or are you engaging Edgar, the erudite professor? Fix on a workable number—I would suggest a maximum of four main avatars to get you started. The avatars are supposed to help you decide, not overwhelm you with too much choice.

Keep these imaginary friends at the top of your mind as you create and connect. Would Felicity love this plot twist? How can you engage Ivan? Would the jokes for Clara hit the same as your lines to intrigue Edgar? Tailor writing and marketing to delight your dream patrons.

Although they are archetypes and not actual people, your avatars may evolve over time. Like all siblings, as they grow, they'll need more space—ideally their own room. Some might even want to leave home and explore the sights and sounds of a new type of story. Does that mean you have to redecorate? Do you follow them with new books in a new genre under a

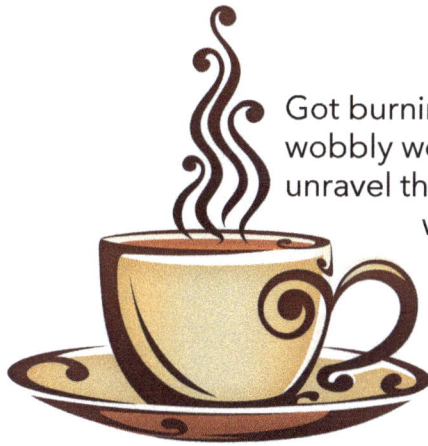

Got burning questions about the wibbly-wobbly world of indie authoring? Eager to unravel the mysteries of publishing, writing woes, or anything in between? Give your quizzical quills a whirl and shoot your musings over to indieannie@ indieauthormagazine.com. Your inky quandaries are my cup of tea!

new pen name? Or do you let them fly and focus on the avatars who remain? Perhaps you might even want to recruit a new avatar to take their place. The important thing is to review your audience constantly and adjust your avatar family accordingly.

Next, identify any running themes that thread across their rooms. For example, Stephen King terrifies readers of all ages who crave creepy tales with relatable characters. Ann Patchett transports book club gal pals to vivid global settings through family dramas.

In short, what is your brand, and how does it satisfy your audience? Different avatars will have different tastes, but with careful attention to detail in your design, you can offer something to please them all.

As with all good writing, avoid clichés. Cozy Mysteries do have readers who knit and bake, but they aren't all grannies that live on the East Coast. Think instead of how books about knitting grannies on the East Coast who solve ghastly murders appeal to different demographics within your reader pool. What is it about your stories that draw people in?

Defining your ideal reader offers many concrete benefits for writing and marketing.

Craft more resonant stories: You can tailor your plots, characters, themes, and voice to intrigue those most keen for your tales.

Streamline marketing: Target ads and promos to places your ideal audience already hangs out, whether book clubs, niche blogs, or related fan communities.

Attract true superfans: Those who love your style will buy, review, and promote your work, fueling word-of-mouth buzz.

Establish expertise: You can become a big fish in your niche rather than getting lost in the vast ocean of broad genres.

Boost engagement: You'll interact with readers you deeply understand. They'll feel seen and develop loyalty.

Clarify branding: Create cohesive covers and messaging that will attract your tribe instantly.

Inspire your muse: Writing for a well-defined audience you can envision will elevate your craft and joy.

Simplify social media: Promote where your people thrive and share content specifically tailored for them.

Clarify your plans: Ideal reader profiles can influence productive career decisions.

Defining your target audience takes work but pays creative and commercial dividends. I hope these benefits convey why the time spent getting to know your imaginary friends is well worth the effort. Now craft a dream house for them, and watch your fan base flourish.

Happy writing,
Indie Annie

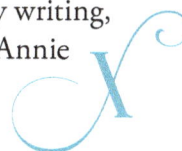

10 TIPS FOR
THE PARA METHOD

As an indie author, your imagination is boundless, conjuring fantastical worlds, intricate plots, and memorable characters. Yet the reality of managing your indie author business often paints a different picture—one of a cluttered desk and digital spaces teeming with disparate ideas, scattered notes, endless to-do lists, and burgeoning files of research materials and marketing plans. This constant influx of information and tasks can quickly transform your creative haven into a daunting battlefield of overwhelm, where finding a crucial piece of research or that brilliant note about a plot twist feels akin to searching for a needle in a haystack.

Enter the PARA Method, a beacon of clarity in the chaotic storm of information management. Conceived by productivity expert Tiago Forte, the PARA Method offers a robust yet flexible framework designed to streamline your workflow and elevate your productivity to new heights. PARA, an acronym for projects, areas, resources, and archives, is an organizational system and mindset shift in one, allowing you to sort the pieces of your digital life and better manage the plethora of information integral to your role as an indie author.

Projects are defined as a series of tasks bound by a common goal and timeline. Each book you write, each marketing campaign you plan, and each book launch you orchestrate falls into this category. Projects are dynamic and demand your immediate attention; they're the front lines, where the action happens.

Areas are components of your professional and creative life that require ongoing maintenance and attention. These include your writing—across genres and series—your brand as an indie author, continuous marketing efforts, and engagement with your readership. Unlike projects, areas don't have an endpoint; they grow with your career.

Resources encompass the information you collect and refer to over time. This can range from research on historical periods for your novels and character development workshops to compilations of marketing strategies and analytics. Resources are your library, the wellspring of knowledge you draw from to enrich your writing and business acumen.

Archives serve as the final resting place for projects and information that are no longer active but might be needed in the future. Completed book series, past marketing campaigns, and outdated research are archived, keeping them out of your immediate workspace but accessible if the need arises.

Implementing the PARA Method begins with a survey of your current digital and physical workspace. Identifying and categorizing your existing tasks and information into these four distinct buckets can illuminate your immediate priorities, simplify decision making, and significantly reduce the time spent searching for files and notes. By allocating a designated space for each category, you create a structured environment where creativity can flourish unimpeded by the chaos of disorganization.

Read on for more tips to incorporate the PARA Method into your author business.

1 IDENTIFY AND TAME YOUR ACTIVE PROJECTS

The first step to utilizing the PARA Method is acknowledging the projects currently vying for your attention. List everything, from that first draft simmering on your laptop to the marketing plan you keep putting off. Here's where PARA's infamous "Ten-to-Fifteen-Project Rule" comes in. Studies suggest our brains struggle to manage more than ten to fifteen active projects effectively, so be ruthless. Prioritize your top projects, and consider putting the rest on hold or delegating them if possible.

2 CHOOSE YOUR WEAPON

Choose where you'd like to organize each category—and subcategory—of PARA going forward. Although there are many note-taking and organizational systems to choose from, Notion's project management features can be a game changer for indie authors. Create a dedicated workspace for each project, complete with to-do lists, deadlines, and even embedded research materials from your "resources" section. Notion's Kanban boards can also offer a visual representation of your project progress, keeping you motivated and on track.

Other systems offer similar structures, such as Todoist's projects, which can be set up with a similar structure. It's worth testing to see which platform makes your life easier and incorporates your current tech stack most effectively.

3 DEFINE YOUR ONGOING RESPONSIBILITIES

"Areas" represent the ongoing tasks that keep your authorial life humming. This could be social media engagement, manuscript revisions, or writers' conferences. Define these areas clearly, and establish routines for tackling them. For instance, dedicate a specific time slot each week for social media interaction, or schedule regular editing sprints.

Pro Tip: If you're using project management software, create dedicated sections or databases for each area. For example, a social media database could track post ideas, scheduled tweets, and follower engagement metrics.

4 CURATE YOUR INSPIRATION

Use the PARA Method to fill your creative fuel tank. Gather your reference materials under the "resources" umbrella. This could be anything from character profiles and world-building notes to inspirational articles and competitor research. Keep your resources organized by project or area for easy retrieval. When you're writing, you now have a categorized library of inspiration to browse if your idea well starts to run dry.

Pro Tip: Bookmark inspirational articles directly into your workspace using Google Chrome Extensions for Notion, Pinterest, or Evernote. Upload character profiles, research documents, and audio recordings of interviews.

(5) DON'T TRASH; JUST STASH

Don't confuse "archives" with a trash bin. Completed projects and outdated resources deserve a respectful retirement home. Store them neatly in your archive for future reference. You never know when a seemingly irrelevant detail from an old project might spark a brilliant new idea.

Pro Tip: While PARA is intended to bring all your information into one space, you can also employ these methods in your email app too. Use the archive method to keep important emails for reference as needed. There's no need to label or add to folders for this one; just use the search feature to locate what you need.

(6) UTILIZE A HOLDING ZONE

Not everything falls neatly into one of the PARA categories. Maybe you stumbled upon a fascinating writing prompt you're not ready to tackle yet or an interesting marketing strategy you want to explore later. Create a temporary holding zone for these undecided items, a sort of "maybe later" list. Review this zone periodically and decide whether to assign these items to a specific project, add them to your resources, or simply archive them.

(7) SCHEDULE DEDICATED PARA PROCESSING TIME

The key to PARA's success is consistent and dedicated use. Don't try to categorize everything on the fly. Schedule regular "PARA processing sessions" to review and organize your information and tasks. This could be a weekly review where you sift through recent additions to your holding zone, check the progress of ongoing projects, and update your archives. Treat these sessions like a sacred ritual—uninterrupted time where you refine your workflow and ensure everything is in its right place. By dedicating specific times to this process, you'll prevent the buildup of miscellaneous information that can lead to overwhelm.

(8) LEVERAGE DIGITAL TOOLS FOR SEAMLESS INTEGRATION

In today's digital age, using the right tools can significantly enhance your productivity and the effectiveness of the PARA Method. Use apps like Zapier or IFTTT to automate the movement of information across your platforms. For instance, automatically save email attachments to a specific Google Drive folder designated for resources, or use applets to add tasks to your projects list on Notion from your email. This seamless integration not only saves time but also ensures that you capture and categorize important information as it comes in.

⑨ ENGAGE WITH YOUR ARCHIVES

View your archives not just as a storage unit but as a gold mine of past experiences and ideas. Schedule monthly or quarterly reviews of your archives to rediscover content that can be repurposed or inspire new projects. This active engagement can turn what was once considered dead content into something vibrant and relevant, reinforcing the cyclical nature of creativity and productivity.

---

⑩ CULTIVATE A MINDSET OF FLEXIBILITY AND ADAPTATION

The ultimate strength of the PARA Method lies not in its structure but in its flexibility. Cultivate a mindset that embraces change and adaptation. As projects evolve, areas of focus shift, and resources become outdated, be willing to reevaluate and reorganize your categories. This mindset ensures that your organizational system grows and adapts with you, supporting your dynamic authorial journey and enabling sustained productivity and creativity.

Adopting the PARA Method as an indie author can lead to embracing a structured yet flexible approach to manage the multitude of tasks and information that come with the territory. By following these tips and making the PARA Method a cornerstone of your workflow, you can transform the overwhelming chaos into a streamlined, productive environment where your creativity thrives. Remember, the goal is not just to work smarter but also to create a space where your imagination can roam freely, unencumbered by the mundane. Let the PARA Method be your guide to a more organized, productive, and creative authorial journey. ■

Chelle Honiker

Chelle Honiker

Chelle Honiker is an advocate for the empowerment of authorpreneurs, recognizing the importance of authors taking charge of both their craft and careers. In response to this need, she has founded a media and training company dedicated to supporting these creative professionals. As the co-founder and publisher of Indie Author Magazine, IndieAuthorTraining, Indie Author Tools, and Direct2Readers.com, Chelle's team of more than 80 writers, editors, trainers, and support staff provides resources and insights that help authors navigate the complexities of self-publishing. Her role as the programming director for Author Nation, an annual conference in Las Vegas, further exemplifies her commitment to fostering a community where authors can grow and succeed. With a career spanning over two decades in executive operations and leadership, Chelle has honed her skills in managing complex projects and delivering impactful training programs. Her experience as a speaker and TEDx Organizer has taken her to many countries, where she has shared her insights with diverse audiences.

From Nighttime Narratives to Novels

BEN HALE'S UNCONVENTIONAL PATH TO WRITING SUCCESS

Ben Hale never could have imagined that consuming Fantasy tales as an avid young reader would reshape his life. His writing journey sparked from a love of reading, but a well-kept secret that lasted nearly fifteen years has allowed Hale to touch countless lives. Led by his budding imagination, young Hale began conjuring up his own whimsical stories as a bedtime ritual at the age of twelve.

His fascination with mental storytelling groomed his career as an acclaimed YA Sci-Fi, Fantasy, and Action-Adventure author with forty-one books under his belt. Hale's humility and passion for storytelling are evident as he shares pieces of his journey as an unlikely author. Like many indie authors, his story involves the power of perseverance, talent, and a bit of luck while taking the publishing world by storm.

AN UNFORESEEN ROUTE TO SUCCESS

For Hale, the path to success was anything but a straight line. "I was caught reading by flashlight under my covers at night," he reminisces. "I naturally gravitated towards Fantasy. It was just so enchanting."

However, it wasn't until a conversation with his wife one night that Hale realized the potential of his storytelling gift. "She asked me, 'How do you fall asleep so

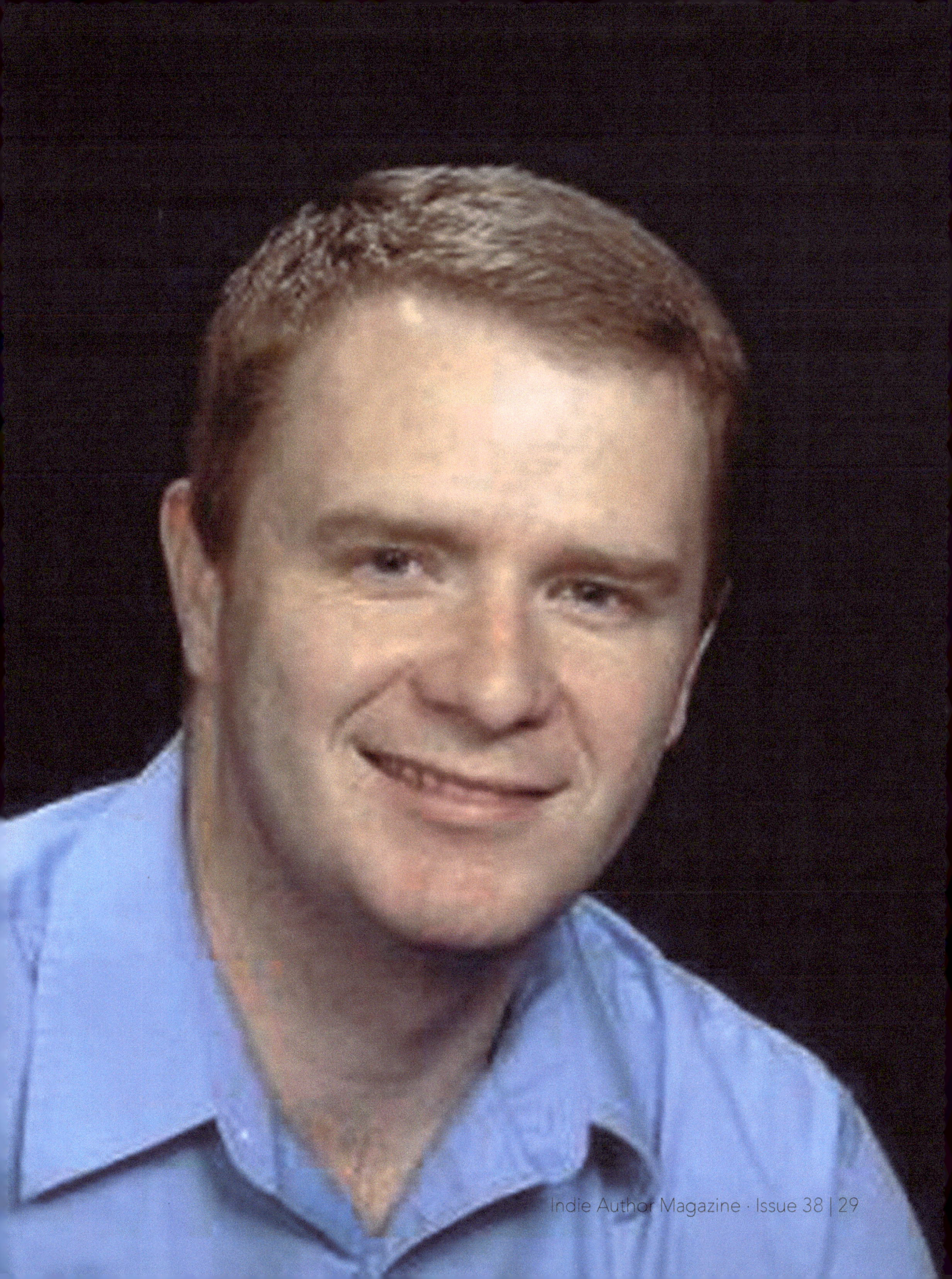

fast every night?' When I told her about the story I'd been making up for the past fifteen years, she said, 'Tell me this story.' And after days of sharing it with her, she urged me to write it down," Hale recalls with a chuckle.

From there, Hale embarked on a journey of creative expression that unfolded more opportunities than he could ever dream. With three books written in just three years, he found himself at a crossroads: traditional publishing or the burgeoning world of indie publishing. "In 2012, I found out about indie publishing, and that really appealed to me," Hale says. "I liked the idea of managing my own work and going after that. That isn't to say I [hadn't] tried to submit because I did and got rejected."

Taking a leap of faith into the indie publishing world, Hale was unaware of the remarkable success that awaited him. "It was a combination of several things and definitely a bit of luck," he reflects. "When I released my books, there wasn't as much competition as there is now. So anyone with a decent or well-written story tended to rise."

And rise he did. Within six months, his earnings skyrocketed past his unassuming goal of $100 a month to an astonishing $10,000. "I stumbled into the right place at the right time," he says, attributing his success to a relentless pursuit of improvement and a genuine passion for his craft. "I consider myself to be a decent writer, but people write [to] me and say that I changed their life. They're reading my books with their kids and they just love it. It's changed who they are, and to be a part of that is just amazing."

> Innovation will always be essential in the writing world and anyone who pushes the boundaries of ideas introduces new genres. It's amazing, and it creates new universes that everybody wants to jump into.
> —Ben Hale

CRAFTING STORIES OF IMPACT

Hale's path to full-time authorship was not without its twists and turns. During a moment of introspection, clad in pajamas and surrounded by the soft glow of his computer screen, he contemplated the trajectory of his writing career. Despite a stable income and the success of his published works, a gentle nudge from within urged him to strive for more.

"I believe it was a prompting from God that said, 'You're capable of more,'" recalls Hale. Seeking to refine his skills and deepen his understanding of the craft, Hale pursued a master's in professional writing—a decision that underscored his commitment to growth and excellence. He didn't do it alone; his wife embarked on the journey alongside him, both of them making the choice amid the whirlwind of a growing family.

"My wife and I always say, 'We do everything better together.' So we decided to pursue our master's degrees together," Hale says, "which is kind of nuts because at that point we had four kids, and number five was on the way. But we said, 'You know what? Let's go do it because we can trade off who has the kids and who's doing classes. We can also do our homework together.' So, we enrolled together, got master's degrees together, and graduated together."

The twists also exist in the intricacies of his series catalog, which consists of a world of interconnected stories and recognizable characters that span storylines and even genre classifications. "With any series [a reader] starts in, I intentionally wrote it where the reader feels like they're exploring this world that overlaps with legacies and crossovers," Hale says. With each installment, Hale weaves in adventure and intrigue, inviting readers to immerse themselves in the vast landscapes of his imagination.

"At the heart of my writing lies the belief that everyone matters. Any character can have an impact on the world: a protective mother, or a courageous child," he says. Through his characters, Hale seeks to illuminate the courage and resilience found within ordinary people who face extraordinary circumstances. From valiant acts of protection to the unexpected journey of a thief with the power to steal concepts, Hale's stories resonate with the notion that greatness can arise from the most unlikely people.

When designing his complex narratives, Hale approaches his projects with a meticulous eye for detail. "I'm definitely a plotter, but it's on a spectrum. I sit down with a vision or idea and the major points and storylines flow from there. As far as my series, I wanted readers to feel like they could start with any one of them and anything else they read afterward feels like a sequel." While he acknowledges the occasional need for cover redesigns to align with contemporary trends, his focus remains on crafting stories that stand the test of time.

Hale receives a first-place Royal Palm Literary Award from the Florida Writers Association in 2013 for his book, The Second Draeken War

When asked his opinion on emerging technologies and trends, like artificial intelligence, Hale says he embraces them with cautious optimism and realism.

"Though it can be controversial at times, I believe that AI will eventually be used in nearly every facet of publishing," he says. "Innovation will always be essential in the writing world and anyone who pushes the boundaries of ideas introduces new genres. It's amazing, and it creates new universes that everybody wants to jump into. ... Before *Twilight*, vampires didn't sparkle, and now they do ... or at least some of them."

CHARTING NEW NARRATIVES

> As writers, we have this enormous, near-unfathomable potential to create. And so if we are willing to give our best now, we must believe that more will come. —Ben Hale

For aspiring authors daunted by getting started, Hale offers simple yet profound advice: embrace courage and perseverance. He offered one of his favorite quotes from British writer and literary scholar C. S. Lewis: "Courage is not simply one of the virtues but the form of every virtue at the testing point, which means at the point of the highest reality." Through his coaching and mentorship of other authors—he keeps a few slots open, he says, to help those who approach him with questions—Hale seeks to inspire others to embrace their creativity and pursue their literary dreams with unwavering determination.

Hale's literary repertoire extends beyond the confines of a single genre. His diverse body of work spans enchanting Fantasy tales, Action-Adventures, and even the heartwarming landscapes of Clean Romance. Hale is unafraid to navigate new territories, giving his readers fresh narrative landscapes. Reflecting on his creative process to share with aspiring authors, Hale emphasizes the importance of giving your all in the present moment. "Hold nothing back in the book you're writing now. As writers, we have this enormous, near-unfathomable potential to create. And so if we are willing to give our best now, we must believe that more will come."

Hale's story serves as an inspiration to aspiring authors everywhere, reminding us that greatness often lies in the quiet courage to pursue our dreams against all odds. As Hale aptly puts it, "While writing my first two books, I didn't tell a soul, besides my wife, for about two years. I was embarrassed because the idea of being a novelist was foreign. I didn't want others to laugh in my face and I fully expected them to say, 'There's no way you can write a book,'" he says. "I hope that inspires aspiring authors who think 'No one will ever be interested in this.' Someone somewhere is yearning to hear your voice because when we write, we provide a connection, an opportunity."

Hale released *Haven of Glass*, the newest book in his The Augment War series, in early April, and the journey ahead brims with promise and excitement. He has several thrilling projects in the works showcasing his genre-spanning versatility and believes his journey can serve as an inspiration for independent authors everywhere. From a nightly dream, he has created books that have uplifted and changed lives. Through his resounding courage, he illuminates a path for generations of storytellers yet to come. ■

Eryka Parker

Hale on an author panel at Indie Bookfest

Eryka Parker

Eryka Parker is a book coach, an award-winning developmental editor, and writing instructor. As a women's contemporary author under the pen name Zariah L. Banks, she creates emotional intimacy novels that prove that everyone deserves to feel seen, appreciated, and loved. She lives in Northeast Ohio with her husband and two children and is currently working on her third novel.

Tapas and Friends: 20Books Sevilla 2024 in Review

Although there's a lot to learn at writing conferences, there are two things that only in-person conferences can provide: the energy found from being among other authors and networking opportunities.

20Books Sevilla took the energy and networking found at most 20BooksTo50K® conferences to a new level. Heidi Heinz, Lola Parrilla Heinz, Enrique Parrilla, and the team at Lantia Publishing put countless hours and effort into making this conference memorable.

Held at the movie theater in Plaza de Armas in the heart of Seville, the two-day conference on March 8 and 9 provided ample opportunities for learning, networking, and enjoying good food and drinks. The conference provided breakfast and lunch each day, and a cash bar was available at the end of the day. Whether you were enjoying food and drinks at the conference or venturing a few blocks away to try different restaurants, see the flamenco dancers, visit the stunning cathedrals, or enjoy an amazing view

Michael Anderle, founder of 20BooksTo50K®, and Enrique Parrilla, event organizer, welcome everyone to the conference Friday, March 8.

of the city from on top of Setas de Sevilla, the city of Seville has something for everyone. I enjoyed the

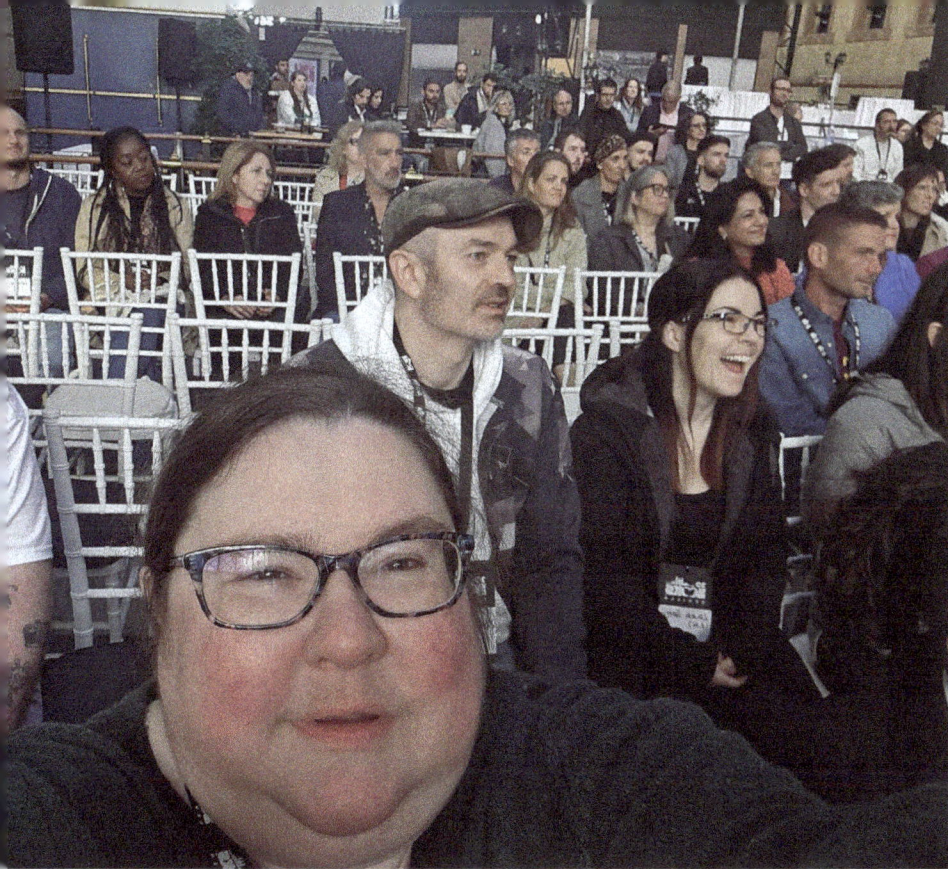

An image of the crowd during the welcome speech March 8.

food, the smell of the orange trees along the sidewalks, and the friendship of fellow authors.

As for the 20Books event that took place there, the front of the program had the words "The how-to for indie authors from around the world: English and Spanish," and it became an accurate description of the conference. I met people from all over Europe and even Canada and the United States at the event. Whether you were in sessions, networking between sessions, or eating and drinking with newfound friends after the conference was done, there was a lot of how-to learning happening. Sessions covered how to use AI tools as part of your author business, writing your marketing into your books, how to use video marketing to increase sales and reach, how to keep your creativity flowing after writing one hundred books, and more. Each session was designed for thirty minutes of speaking and fifteen minutes of questions and answers, with many attendees asking helpful questions that built on what was taught in the session.

But what I found most delightful was the emphasis Parrilla and Heinz put on networking between sessions. Based on feedback from last year's event, they built thirty-minute networking breaks into the schedule between each session, as well as a two-hour lunch, and set up time afterward for networking in the theater. There was plenty of space to spread out and talk in quieter locations if desired, or you could stay with the big group of people. Of course, that continued into the hotel after the conference ended.

With two hundred to three hundred people at this conference, I felt I could meet and get to know people a bit better at the conference than I did at 20Books Vegas events. There were always so many people in Las Vegas who wanted to meet so many of the same people that sometimes it could be overwhelming. However, I never felt overwhelmed by the smaller crowd in Seville. As both a speaker and an attendee, I found the atmosphere to be very welcoming. People were quick to introduce themselves and make friends. Of course, it was good to see faces I already knew, including well-known names in the industry like 20Books-To50K® co-founder Michael Anderle, bestselling author Adam Beswick, host of the *Rebel Author Podcast* Sacha Black, Sci-Fi author Craig Falconer, author and *IAM* columnist Steve Higgs, bestselling Urban Fantasy author Sarah Noffke, speaker and self-improvement author Marc Reklau, host of *The Creative Penn* podcast Joanna Penn, and others, at the conference as well.

Three tracks were held in three theaters each day, two in English and one in Spanish. While a few of the sessions were panels, most featured individual speakers on topics that appealed to all levels of authors.

I can't speak to the Spanish track, but the English tracks offered attendees some important takeaways:

Don't run from your problems, go through them. This was the second time I heard this talk by Noffke, and just like the first time in Las Vegas last year, it struck a chord with me. Far too often, we run from our problems, and this was a good reminder

From left, Steve Higgs, Sarah Noffke, and Sean McLachlan before their panel talk on being part of The Century Club, having written one hundred or more books.

for me to start facing them and defeating them.

If at first you don't succeed, keep trying. I listened to several authors who talked about how their first books didn't work out, or advertising didn't work out the first or even the fifth time they tried, but they kept working on it until they found what worked for them. Now they're teaching what they learned to everyone else.

Know your market. Know why certain marketing tactics work better than others depending on genre, tropes, and your audience. It's more than just writing to market; it's about attracting that audience as well.

Experiment. If something doesn't work, try something new. If it works, don't hesitate to reuse it until it no longer performs.

Learn from others. Just because you are still learning doesn't mean you won't one day be on the stage teaching others what you've learned on your journey.

With this event in the rearview mirror, it's time to look forward to other events in Europe and the United Kingdom, including The Self Publishing Show Live June 25-26 in London and the Author Sustainability Conference April 3-6, 2025, in Dublin, Ireland. Visit https://selfpublishing.lpages.co/sps-live-2024 or https://authorsustainability.com, respectively, to learn more or register, or check out *IAM*'s list of top indie author events for 2024 at https://indieauthormagazine.com/whats-in-store-for-2024. ▪

Grace Snoke

From left, Judith Anderle, Francesco Vitellini, and Jens Schultze answer questions about translating books into other languages.

Grace Snoke

Grace Snoke is a 42-year-old author and personal assistant residing in Lincoln, Nebraska. Having been a corporate journalist for more than a decade and a video game journalist for even longer, writing has been something she has always enjoyed doing. In addition to non-fiction books, she is currently working on a paranormal romance series, and two urban fantasy series under her real name. She has also released more than a dozen illustrated children's books and several non-fiction books. She has been publishing erotica under a pen name since 2017. For more information about her personal assistant business visit: https://spiderwebzdesign.net. Her author site is: https://gracesnoke.com.

Let the Games Begin

MARKETING LESSONS CHILDREN'S BOOK AUTHORS CAN LEARN FROM THE 2024 OLYMPIC GAMES

France is making its final preparations for the Olympic Games next month. Stadiums have been erected around famous sites in Paris, including the Eiffel Tower and the Palace of Versailles, so that historic shots of winning athletes will have cultural icons as backdrops. Capitalizing on French cultural sites will probably drive the Parisians mad, but it's a magical example of both using what you have and giving a project an elegant frame.

Both mindsets can also be perfect guidelines for how children's book authors can approach marketing, which, coincidentally, should also kick off around this time of year for authors hoping to get serious about holiday sales. Reviewing what you already have—deleted scenes, coloring pages, worksheets, or character sketches—and where your work could fit in—comparable titles, tie-ins to current events and festivals, or connections to existing bookstore or library campaigns—can set you and your business up for sustainable success.

Want more tips for marketing children's books? Here's how you can give your publishing strategy that Parisian touch.

GO FOR CACHET

Follow the French example and lend your books cachet by applying early for prestigious awards and editorial reviews. The magic ingredient here is allowing a four- to six-month window after the book is complete before publication. To start your search, the Alliance of Independent Authors (ALLi) has a vetted database of book awards and contests open to indie authors in a range of genres, found at https://selfpublishingadvice.org/author-awards-contests-rated-reviewed. The organization also published an e-book, *Book Prizes & Awards for Indie Authors*, available in the ALLi bookshop (https://selfpublishingadvice.org/bookshop) for free to members. Another option is a free or paid membership to Book Award Pro (https://bookawardpro.com), a site that curates a custom list of awards opportunities for your title. Enter the details for each of your books, and receive suggestions via email.

"Go for respect," says Darcy Pattison, award-winning children's author and owner of the independent publisher Mims House. She uses awards to prove that her books meet educational standards and to show how they fit into curricula. Applying for awards is a regular part of publishing for Pattison, whose official "awards season" ends in July. Her launch plan for indie authors of children's books, available through her Substack, has suggestions for book awards, editorial reviews, and timing.

Once your books have cachet, they need to flaunt it. For the Rugby World Cup held in France in 2023, posh tourist assistance offices—la boutique, officially—sprang up in train stations in ten different cities, sporting cushy red benches, extra staff to ensure

a positive train experience, and adorable bookmarks cut in the shape of a high-speed French Train à Grande Vitesse. If your book earned an award, add the graphic to your website; consider a gold seal for the print editions; and add the "sell quote" from an editorial review to your book covers, book descriptions, or front matter. Make a bookmark of your own. Like the World Cup's miniature paper train, your bookmark can glide across the desk as a souvenir of a never-to-be-forgotten adventure, or as the promise of a book that will delight readers and bookstore owners alike.

TREAT YOUR PARTNERS WITH PANACHE

France's communication plan for the Olympic Games might be more than you need, but a classy bookmark, a catalog, or a sell sheet could be just the ticket for keeping your books top of mind at ordering time. You've crafted an experience for your readers and set it off with an excellent cover and description. Now make something to remember it by, perhaps a prop to spark word-of-mouth recommendations.

Retailers, educational and library distributors, subscription services, and editorial reviewers all understand your book's target market more quickly when they have context. Pattison's website includes a downloadable catalog of Mims House titles to share with distributors, and she uses "sell sheets" to pitch individual titles to schools and libraries. "Children's books don't sell the same places in the same ways as adult books," Pattison says. "If you ask a children's librarian at a school library, 'Where do you buy books?' They buy from education distributors because their school has an account set up with them already." The two biggest, she says, are Follett and Mackin, and worth exploring for indie authors looking to target a school-age audience of readers.

SPORT YOUR CREATIVITY

France wants to "reward creativity and athletic performance" with four new sports in 2024: breaking, sport climbing, skateboarding, and surfing, in an effort to serve young people. How could you serve a new audience or market with

your work? Innovations in tools, formats, distributors, or markets could mean new sales records for indie publishers, but only if they perceive the new opportunities.

Through reading *Publishers Weekly*, Pattison found a premier reading app for schools called Epic! and got in on the ground floor. She understood the advantage of Epic!'s business model before it was proven in the arena. "Epic! is free for schools," Pattison says, "so 80 to 90 percent of US schools have it, but parents have to buy it." Currently, a publisher needs fifty books to be eligible for Epic!, but Pattison's reward for taking a risk on an unknown platform was huge. One of her titles, *A Little Bit of Dinosaur*, has over a million reads on the platform. In another creative publishing move, Pattison created pop-up technology books that sported her award-winning quilting skills.

How can you expand into new markets or formats? Some examples are more obvious than others, but don't be afraid to stray down new paths to see where they lead. In *IAM*'s May 2024 issue, ALLi Campaigns Manager Melissa Addey details the outlet some children's book authors have found in Yoto cards (https://uk.yotoplay.com) allowing parents and grandparents to create personalized audiobooks of their titles for young readers.

PLAN FOR A MAINTENANCE PHASE

Win or lose, when this year's athletes return from the Olympic Games, they'll take time to review their performances to see where they can improve. Off-season training could lead to a breakthrough. This summer, take time to review what's working for your books. When you're updating your shiny catalog or marketing materials, it's the perfect time to perfect your routines. What's working? Do more of that. What other skills, passions, and interests do you have outside of writing? Use them as a backdrop to give your books allure by association. Update your talking points to include new insights about audience appeal, review quotes, or new awards. Organic, steady, and creative growth can be sustainable for your publishing business.

By tradition, the Olympic Games are for amateurs, but many "retired" Olympic athletes take on professional and paid employment using their world-class skills. The publishing equivalent is the sale of intellectual property (IP). Indie authors spend more time in front of screens than the average Olympic athlete, but most indie authors write for love before they write for money. Andy Weir famously published *The Martian* in installments on his blog, then went pro on Kindle when readers requested an e-book. Since then, he sold audiobook rights to Podium Publishing, then the print rights to Random House's Crown Publishing.

But before you decide that the Olympic Games of publishing are only for rocket books, consider Pattison's experience as a children's author. After creating and publishing a large body of work, she has discovered what matters to her and is going pro at a higher level to get her themes, topics, and stories out into the world.

"I have a book with a million reads," she says. "I have other books with great awards. I have now sixty-five books … [and] some interesting intellectual property. So how can I translate that to something else for kids?" For her, it's time "to look around at adjacent industries that serve kids to see if there [are] opportunities or not."

Halfway through the year is the perfect time to garner cachet for your existing creations, parlez-vous your way into some opportunities you may have overlooked, push toward the goal with some new stretch goals, and publish with panache. Pay attention to these, and you'll be on your game. ■

Laurel Decher

Laurel Decher

There might be no frigate like a book, but publishing can feel like a voyage on the H.M.S. Surprise. There's always a twist and there's never a moment to lose. Laurel's mission is to help you make the most of today's opportunities. She's a strategic problem-solver, tool collector, and co-inventor of the "you never know" theory of publishing. As an epidemiologist, she studied factors that help babies and toddlers thrive. Now she writes books for children ages nine to twelve about finding more magic in life. She's a member of the Society for Children's Book Writers and Illustrators (SCBWI), has various advanced degrees, and a tendency to smuggle vegetables into storylines.

What the Machines Have Learned

UPGRADE YOUR MARKETING WITH AI INITIATIVES

Last year, *Indie Author Magazine* focused an entire issue on AI, the ways authors could make use of new machine learning platforms, and some of the ethical concerns involved with the impact of artificial intelligence on the publishing industry. Since then, the opportunities and challenges have continued to expand.

In her article "(Artificially) Intelligent Advertising," *IAM* staff writer Gayle Leeson discussed using Sudowrite, Jasper.ai, or the AI editors available through platforms like SocialBee and Wix Facebook Ads to develop marketing and social media copy. She also delved into the, at the time, limited use of AI for market research and highlighted Marlowe (https://authors.ai/marlowe), an application that offers manuscript critiques.

All of those options are still available. Indeed, SocialBee now labels the company an "AI-Powered Social Media Management Tool" in their SEO. But these programs and more have evolved considerably in the past year, becoming even more powerful in the wake of 2023's AI boom. So how can authors get the most out of AI tools for marketing and promotional strategies in 2024?

USING GENERATIVE AI

Since you may already be familiar with ChatGPT—I gave you ten tips for writing better prompts last year—here are some ways to use it for marketing, recommended by Book Launchers in a blog post for IngramSpark. Try uploading your manuscript and asking the AI to create articles, podcast scripts, or other content. Although at first glance it seems like this would be more useful for nonfiction writers, authors of fiction could also upload portions of their manuscript and test the AI's ability to write blurb variations or rewrite a scene from an alternate point-of-view for use as a newsletter bonus or other reader magnet. The blog author includes the caveat that you'll still want to edit the output, but since the AI starts with something you've already created, the content should be stronger. Other suggestions include asking your AI for more content ideas and asking for ways to market your book. Book Launchers also recommends asking your AI to do research on influencers, bookstores, or libraries for you. You can get ChatGPT or Jasper to generate a list of YouTube channels or blogs that relate to your book's topic or genre, quickly providing you a list of people to contact for potential collaborations or networking.

BEYOND CONTENT

In December 2023, Lisa Harkness, Kelsey Robinson, Eli Stein, and Winnie Wu published an article, "How generative AI can boost consumer marketing," for strategy and management consulting firm McKinsey & Company. They identified the following examples as ways AI "has the potential to deliver value quickly": personalization of marketing campaigns, unstructured customer data analysis, process automation, and opportunity identification and idea generation. Ironically, all four AI initiatives are used by large retailers like Michaels, Stitch Fix, and Mattel to humanize users' experiences with their online stores and deepen engagement.

The authors recommend limiting AI tools to these specific purposes because "attempting to incorporate too many different [generative] AI initiatives in the hope that something sticks can end up being costly, diffuse, and difficult to track, making it hard to incorporate whatever lessons are generated across the launches."

Alisha Lyndon, of *Forbes*, writes, "It's important to keep in mind that generative AI is about reshuffling tasks, not replacing jobs. In other words, it should be set to augment, not substitute." With that in mind, she offers more ideas for using AI to create a more personal connection with your customers—or readers, in the case of your author business.

First, she suggests using AI's "prowess in analyzing datasets and recognizing patterns" to scale personalization by prioritizing accounts. This might mean segmenting your newsletter list or streamlining your funnels to deliver more individualized experiences for your readers. Once you have your audience sorted, you can further tailor your content to individual readers using generative AI to create deeper engagement.

If you want to test reader responses to new content before you roll it out, Lyndon writes that you can use AI to build a sandbox in which to stress-test those reactions. By giving the AI information on your readers, you can ask it to predict what content, style, or tone might work best with that group of people. You can also use AI-driven analytics to "identify the next best actions for high-value accounts." This way, you can focus your energy where it will have the greatest impact.

Unite.ai, a website that specializes in providing news about progress on AI, recently released a series of reports on the Mobile World Congress (MWC) Conference, including a panel on "unleashing creativity through the human-robot duality in marketing." Although their coverage starts with tools for brainstorming and drafting, similar to the previously discussed uses for ChatGPT, the article goes on to explore other ways AI can impact marketing, including helping you find your ideal readers.

According to Jacob Stoner, who wrote the article, one of the most significant advances in the strategic role of AI has been its "ability to analyze and leverage big data with unprecedented accuracy." Because AI

can now identify the most accurate user base for testing, marketing campaigns can become much more targeted. AI technologies like predictive analytics and machine learning can track market trends and consumer behaviors. They can also forecast future shifts and dissect "consumer feedback and online interactions to refine marketing messages and tactics," Stoner writes. These efficiencies allow marketers, and authors, to focus on strategic and creative work.

AI TOOLS FOR AUTHORS

With so many possibilities available, and more on the horizon, it can be challenging to know where to begin. Authors just starting to explore how AI might serve their business may want to choose one or two systems that have already proven themselves in the indie author community.

Here are a few tools to check out if you're ready to move past ChatGPT and MidJourney.

Zapier

Zapier provides integrations for web applications that use automated workflows. For example, Zapier can pair with Google Docs, Trello, Slack, Asana, and Airtable databases, as well as ChatGPT and Writer, another generative AI platform. Authors can input data into a Google form and use Zapier to pass that information to ChatGPT for content generation. Zapier can then transfer the formatted results to Google Docs to be edited. Zapier bills monthly at four levels, depending on the number of tasks you think you'll need, ranging from a $19.99 starter plan to $69 for teams. The free plan features a visual editor and unlimited two-step zaps.

IAM Publisher Chelle Honiker shared a few ways authors can use a combination of Zapier and ChatGPT to automate content creation for social media. After brainstorming with ChatGPT to create a list of subjects and previews for future blog posts, she builds a daisy chain of zaps to draft the blog, create social media posts, craft an image using DALL-E, start a WordPress post using the image and keywords, and load the RSS feed into a newsletter. The resulting content will be optimized for SEO with strong keywords and backlinks. You can even

include a step in the chain that asks Zapier to send the content to a spreadsheet with a checkbox and wait for approval before it pushes the results out to your socials.

Custom GPTs

If you start with one of Open AI's custom GPTs, Honiker says, you can feed the AI a PDF of previous blog posts, or even your manuscript, and get results that mimic your tone and voice. In her experience, only about 20 percent of the resulting blog content needs to be revised. This allows you to create blogs, social media posts, and newsletter content trained on your writing alone.

Pushing the custom GPT further, if you've uploaded your manuscript and given it capabilities for web browsing and image creation, you can ask the AI to develop Amazon blurbs and keywords or craft images for ads and other marketing. Ask it to create a CSV file that lists your characters and the chapters in which they appear, and you have the beginnings of a story bible that you can use in your writing or for reference when you're looking for specific quotes. Prepare for book talks or create a list of discussion questions for your back matter by asking the GPT to analyze your manuscript for tropes and themes. Ultimately, the GPT can create anything you ask it to, so if you run out of ideas, or need guidance in telling it what to do, you can ask it for help.

Shimmr

Shimmr.ai is a UK-based marketing company that uses AI to automate advertising specifically for authors. Using the publisher's EPUB file, its AI develops ads, book descriptions, keywords, and author bios, selects placements to reach the ideal reader, and directs traffic to your sales platform. Shimmr is open to any genre, fiction or nonfiction. Although authors can choose to stop or remove ads at any point, they are deployed automatically after a review of the first round. Shimmr's FAQ section assures partners that "The ePUB is used to create our ads but does not become part of the training set of the LLM." The service is priced at a flat $75 per month, per title in an annual subscription. The CEO, Nadim Sadek, has also published a book on how publishing can embrace AI, titled *Shimmer, Don't Shake*.

As AI continues to expand its capabilities, indie authors may find more of the frustrating tasks of publishing taken completely off their to-do lists, allowing them to focus on the creative work that only humans can do. In the meantime, these tools can upgrade some of the processes you already have in place.

How are you using AI as a tool for market research in your author business? Are there any tools or platforms we've missed that deserve a spotlight? Let us know at feedback@indieauthormagazine.com! ■

Jenn Lessmann

Jenn Lessmann

Jenn Lessmann is the author of Unmagical: a Witchy Mystery and three stories on Kindle Vella. A former barista, stage manager, and high school English teacher with advanced degrees from impressive colleges, she continues to drink excessive amounts of caffeine, stay up later than is absolutely necessary, and read three or four books at a time. Jenn is currently studying witchcraft and the craft of writing, and giggling internally whenever they intersect. She writes snarky paranormal fantasy for new adults whenever her dog will allow it.

Tried-and-True Methods for Marketing Nonfiction

Writing your book was the hard part—or at least that's what you might've thought. But now comes an even harder part: promoting it. Marketing can pose a challenge for any author, but nonfiction authors sometimes have a harder time reaching and connecting with their target audience than even fiction authors do.

Some of the best methods for genre fiction don't translate to true-to-life memoirs or informational guides. Still, making that connection is vital to building your readership and boosting sales. There are many resources nonfiction writers can look to when connecting with their ideal readers, including normal promotion avenues, but some are more suited to nonfiction authors than others.

Whether you are new to writing nonfiction and are looking for your niche or you're an established author hoping to widen your readership, let's explore a few options for establishing yourself as a spokesperson in your target market—and for promoting your books once you've done so.

YOUR OWN WEBSITE

While having an author website is important for fiction authors, it's equally important, if not more so, for nonfiction authors. A website allows you not only to showcase your book but also to compile articles and blog posts you have written on the topic that demonstrate your expertise. In addition, it's a place to build your mailing list, link to media coverage of you or your book, and give readers a way to contact you. It also provides a place to share what you are up to and advertise any events where you will be appearing.

Once you have the initial site set up, consider running ads to your website from Facebook or Google. This allows you to increase your visibility and attract people to your website who are looking for you or information on your topic. Many readers of nonfiction like to look up the authors of the book they've read to see what other books or articles they may have on the topic.

WRITING

ARTICLES OR BLOGS

You are an expert in the topics you have written books about—or, at the very least, you should be. Most likely, you have more content than you have put in your book, or perhaps additional information has become available since you published. These extra prompts and drafts are perfect opportunities for promoting your work and hooking new readers by proving to them your knowledge of the topic.

Authors can sometimes find freelance writing gigs or even work as columnists for newspapers, magazines, or websites. These opportunities give you a chance to get your name and biography listed in publications. In some cases, those biographies can mention the name of your book or that you're an author, as well as your website, where readers can then find out more about you and your book.

It is important to research publications where you are considering submitting to make sure they are a good match for the topic and the readers you want to attract. If it is a regular publication, consider subscribing and reading current and past articles. Their website may also have submission guidelines or an open submissions policy. There is also a website, Where to Pitch (https://wheretopitch.com), which can help you find websites and publications that would be a good match for your topic and are open to pitches.

If you can't find information on submissions with any of these methods, it's best to reach out to the editor of the publication about whether they would be open to accepting pitches for articles. Contact information for most editors can be found within the publication or on the publication's website. If they say yes, pitch some ideas, and if they're accepted, write them and send them their way.

Be sure to ask for and follow their style guides when you write, and listen to their feedback. Afterward, you can ask if they'd be interested in other articles or even an ongoing column.

If you don't have publications in mind, look at freelance sites and see if you can find someone looking for an article in your area of expertise. Some sites to consider include Upwork, Working In Content, Problogger, Be A Freelance Blogger, and Freelance Writing Gigs, though there are plenty more.

Beyond writing for other publications, publishing blog posts on your own site can draw people to your site and potentially more readers to your book. Although some authors can get away with posting one time a week, it's best to post three to five times a week. Posting on a regular schedule helps

readers know when to expect new blog posts, so they can develop a routine around revisiting your site to read them.

SOCIAL MEDIA

Facebook, Twitter, TikTok, and Instagram are a great way to connect with existing readers and new ones. Each platform has its advantages, but the good news is, in many cases, you can reuse content across several platforms. Remember marketing's "rule of seven": people have to see content at least seven times before they'll consider it overused.

Facebook Groups can be a great place to let others know about your book or to share knowledge about the topics you know the most about. There are many groups out there, so be sure to check out the group rules—some don't allow self-promotion—as well as how active members are. If a group hasn't seen much activity, it may not be worth your time to post in it. You might also consider creating your own Facebook Group to share knowledge and promote discussion on those topics. You can even invite other authors who write on the same topic to join and contribute as well.

Reaching out to appropriate BookTokkers and Bookstagrammers is another way to promote your book. Many of them will provide video reviews or create promotional images to share your book when they review it. It is important to remember that some of those promoters will want to be paid in addition to receiving a copy of your book, so keep that in mind when you reach out to them.

Don't forget to use your own social media platforms to promote your books as well. In addition to ads, creating and engaging with your following helps you to spread the word about yourself and your book, and to establish you as an authority figure in your field of expertise. There, you can also share reviews and videos from any influencers with your own followers, increasing your reach—and theirs—even more.

PODCASTS

Similar to reaching out to editors about writing articles for them, reaching out to podcasters about a guest appearance is a great way to not only provide them with an interview for their show but also allow you to find new readers who may not have heard from you before.

Chances are you have some podcasters you listen to regularly who might be perfect for you to pitch to about being on their podcast. If you don't, you may find relevant podcasts on Spotify, Apple, or other platforms. Learn more about the process for becoming a guest on podcasts with *IAM*'s March 2024 feature, "Unlocking the Power of Podcast Appearances for Authors." Most hosts list contact information on the podcast description page or a website. If they are looking for guests, send them a pitch regarding what you want to talk about on their show.

It is important to note that you should find podcasters who have listeners who would be interested in your topic. It's also important to consider whether they're likely to invite guests to speak against your topic, especially if the focus of your book could be controversial. Of course, in these instances, you may want to be on a show to provide your perspective; alternatively, you may want to pass if you are looking to avoid the negativity that could follow such an engagement. Do your research, and consider your options carefully before reaching out to anyone.

PUBLIC EVENTS AND MEDIA INTERVIEWS

In a world focused more and more on technology and connection through online channels, some of the more personal ways to interact with new readers may occur face to face, either through media interviews or in-person events. However, finding places to speak about a topic may require a bit more legwork.

For in-person events and public speaking opportunities, look at professional organizations connected to your subject area, conventions, or conferences that would potentially hold sessions about your expertise to see if they have a call for speakers. If you're interested in exploring this route, it's a good idea to have a place on your website where event organizers can see where you've spoken before, if you have, and if you're open to speaking engagements.

Being open to media interviews is another way to promote yourself. Reporters are always looking for interesting local people to talk about. As an author with an interesting or timely book release, they may be interested in interviewing you. It never hurts to reach out to radio, TV, or even local newspapers to see if they'd be interested in a local feature story about you. It can be as simple as sending them press releases about a new release, sending them an email telling them about yourself and your books and letting them know you'd be open to a local interest piece or interview, or asking a local friend to reach out to them to talk about why they think you'd make an interesting feature piece.

NEWSLETTER SWAPS

Whether you write fiction or nonfiction, reaching out to other authors who have books on the same or similar topics and asking them to promote your book via a newsletter swap is a great way to reach additional

readers. You can organize these using services like StoryOrigin or Book-funnel, but don't be shy about reaching out to authors directly either. Sharing each other's work with a new mailing list can be beneficial to you both. More importantly, you'll be creating connections within the industry that could provide you with future promotion opportunities down the road.

OTHER IDEAS

As many readers as there are for your book, there are even more ways to reach them. If you are looking for more ideas for how to promote your nonfiction books, check out these additional resources:

- *Writer's Digest*, "15 Promotional Ideas for Nonfiction Authors": https://www.writersdigest.com/write-better-nonfiction/15-promotional-ideas-for-nonfiction-authors
- Reedsy blog, "How to Market a Nonfiction Book: 5 Steps to Selling More Books": https://blog.reedsy.com/how-to-market-a-nonfiction-book
- BookBub, "16 Creative Ways Authors Promote Nonfiction Books on Instagram": https://insights.bookbub.com/nonfiction-instagram-book-marketing-ideas
- Elite Authors, "How to Market a Nonfiction Book": https://eliteauthors.com/blog/how-to-market-a-nonfiction-book ■

Grace Snoke

Grace Snoke

Grace Snoke is a 42-year-old author and personal assistant residing in Lincoln, Nebraska. Having been a corporate journalist for more than a decade and a video game journalist for even longer, writing has been something she has always enjoyed doing. In addition to nonfiction books, she is currently working on a paranormal romance series, and two urban fantasy series under her real name. She has also released more than a dozen illustrated children's books and several non-fiction books. She has been publishing erotica under a pen name since 2017. For more information about her personal assistant business visit: https://spiderwebzdesign.net. Her author site is: https://gracesnoke.com.

Everything under the Sunburst

SCRIBECOUNT BRINGS YOUR SALES DATA ACROSS RETAILERS INTO ONE PLACE

For authors who publish wide, tracking sales and trends across different platforms can be time consuming, yet the data it provides can be essential to creating effective marketing strategies. Scribe-Count (https://scribecount.com) offers a way to track and compare sales across several distribution platforms. The online platform can help indie authors collect all their sales data in one application and then, with its selection of built-in features, allow them to make the best decisions for their business using accurate reports. From tracking ads to convenient visualization tools, ScribeCount offers a robust toolset designed and managed by and for indie authors.

ScribeCount connects to various distributors and sales reporting services using a browser extension, which augments the functionality of your current browser. "This extension is like hiring your own personal doorman who will control who and what you wish ScribeCount to see," according to ScribeCount's website. "Unlike other reporting services, this doorman works for you and controls what data goes in and out your door." ScribeCount also states that the application does not visualize or store your passwords, nor can it change any of your data across the platforms it is connected to. The application observes, correlates, compiles, and analyzes the data it is provided through the browser window.

ScribeCount's dashboard can be optimized based on a user's reporting needs, offering a variety of layouts depending on whether you publish hybrid, wide, or direct to Kindle Unlimited. Read on to learn more about ScribeCount's features, tools, and pricing structure so you can decide for yourself if the application has a place in your workflow.

PRICING

ScribeCount aims to be affordable for everyone and offers its entire toolset at any tier level. Tier 1 starts at just $9.99 monthly for authors making less than $1,000 in that time period. ScribeCount only charges more if your income from your sales increases, becoming $19.99 a month for those making over the $1,000 threshold. This monthly charge is variable and will scale down to $9.99 should you not meet the $1,000 threshold, but it will never exceed $19.99 a month. For those who want to save 15 percent, a yearly plan is also available at $185 per year.

If you're interested in testing out ScribeCount, the company offers a two-week free trial, with all features accessible during the trial period.

THE SUNBURST CHART

Visualization of data is an effective way to absorb overall data points without getting lost in the numbers. Connecting different retailers such as Amazon KDP and Barnes & Noble to ScribeCount gives you access to the Sunburst Chart, a pie-chart depiction of your royalties on each platform, in each region, and in each format—print, e-book, and audiobook—even down to the specific book or series. Date ranges are adjustable and make it easy to narrow your focus so you can better understand your business's performance over a given period.

Pro Tip: Most authors look for flexibility and ease of use when it comes to analyzing the data they're provided across multiple platforms. ScribeCount's dashboard is customizable, allowing the user to hide or show features as needed. If you only wish to see one sales channel, click on that section of the ring. You can also select your preferred currency, a specific book across the different channels, or the series across all the channels—and any combination thereof. For authors in Kindle Unlimited, you can set the KU rate, have your chart convert page-reads to sales automatically, and even compare sales to rank by book, series, and marketplace.

AD TRACKING

One of an author's greatest challenges is determining the effectiveness of ad campaigns, judging spend, and evaluating revenue generated, which often includes switching between platforms and managing expansive spreadsheets. ScribeCount's Ad Tracking feature pulls data from Meta and Amazon ads platforms and consolidates it onto your dashboard so you can monitor a campaign without having multiple tabs. Clicks, impressions, spend, and reach are all available to monitor and compare. Authors can also see individual charts offered by ScribeCount, such as Royalties vs. Ad Spend, to assess a campaign's effectiveness.

Pro Tip: Toggle data points in the platform to display your data as a Sunburst Chart, bar graphs, or text using the toggle buttons at the top of the dashboard. Similar buttons are found on the dashboard to help you switch between publishing strategies if you are wide, in Kindle Unlimited, or hybrid.

SPREADSHEETS AND SECURITY

ScribeCount spreadsheets compile multiple data points into a single location, then give authors the flexibility to view and export the data in formats they find most useful. The spreadsheet tool is valuable for traditional data collection, allowing easy export of all aggregated data available on your dashboard. You can filter through columns such as Marketplace, Net Profit, Total Royalties, and Total Expenses, and edit the view to see only what you need.

As a cursory feature, ScribeCount spreadsheets can also combat piracy and help give authors an indication that it's happening via price tracking. Amazon enforces its price-matching policy through web crawls and can spot another e-book offered at another retailer for a reduced price. ScribeCount monitors the prices of your books based on this feature on the distribution site and will notify you of a price change of your books by identifying it on the spreadsheet.

Spreadsheets are excellent tools for data analysis, though authors must be familiar with the data presented and with key terminology, how Kindle Unlimited works, how payouts work, and other facets of publishing to make best use of the features.

HISTORICAL DATA

ScribeCount's data aggregation not only covers current numbers; the application also shows historical sales, page reads, and free titles in a single dashboard, and can pull historical data from pre-set date ranges or a specific reporting period. This feature allows authors to judge the effectiveness of their marketing efforts over time, such as in the instance of a Kindle Daily Deal or limited Barnes & Noble e-book promotions.

Like any tool, overcrowding the dashboard can become a hindrance. ScribeCount thrives on showing you exactly what data you need and allowing you to build out visual reports and spreadsheets from there. Consider starting with one report, digging into the data points, and building onto it from there.

REVIEWS

There is valuable information in reviews, and like sales rankings and revenue generated, reviews are part of an author's business decision-making process. ScribeCount consolidates reviews from every platform and allows filtering and organization by platform, most recent, most positive, and most negative.

CONTINUED IMPROVEMENT

ScribeCount is hard at work integrating new platforms into the existing application. More recent updates have included incorporating sales data from WooCommerce, Shopify, and BookFunnel accounts for those who sell direct with those platforms.

Pro Tip: ScribeCount can generate automatic reports on a regular schedule without you having to drill down to the specific information you need repeatedly. Announced in February 2024, Scribe-Count Analytics received an upgrade to its analytic capabilities and can now run automatic reports. When you provide information about your book, series, and goals, ScribeCount will compile your data in as little as five clicks while walking you through the report. The application contains industry definitions and will output the information in several charts and a spreadsheet.

For those who are new to reports and the terminology but still want to take advantage of the application, ScribeCount contains tutorials built into the system. Each feature of the report contains a text explanation of what it does and how to read it. There are additional links within the application for more in-depth learning. As part of ScribeCount's continued improvement efforts, the company plans to expand the knowledge database over the coming months to offer advice for using ScribeCount from vetted sources in both video and text formats. You can find these tutorials at https://scribecount.com/feature-tours or by tapping "Feature Tours" at the top of the ScribeCount homepage.

A ROBUST TOOL

Although its purpose may seem mundane, Scribe-Count aims to save you time and effort by consolidating information and exporting it in ways that are best for you. Slogging through endless spreadsheets and multiple platforms is the old way of things. ScribeCount is a tool tat can save authors time and money by centralizing that same data in one place and then making it easier to understand. ∎

David Viergutz

David Viergutz

David Viergutz is a disabled Army Veteran, Law Enforcement Veteran, husband and proud father. He is an author of stories from every flavor of horror and dark fiction. One day, David's wife sat him down and gave him the confidence to start putting his imagination on paper. From then on out his creativity has no longer been stifled by self-doubt and he continues to write with a smile on his face in a dark, candle-lit room.

From the Stacks

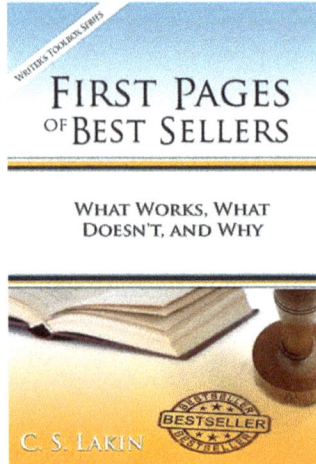

First Pages of Best Sellers: What Works, What Doesn't, and Why
C. S. Lakin
https://indieauthortools.com/books/first-pages-of-best-sellers
Capturing a reader's attention from the first page of a book is crucial to engaging the reader from the onset. It sets the stage for the rest of the story and tells the reader what to expect from that point on, possibly making the difference between the reader purchasing your book and passing it over. *First Pages of Best Sellers* by C. S. Lakin analyzes the first pages of more than two dozen bestselling novels and provides a thorough breakdown of what works, what doesn't, and why. This valuable resource examines topics such as boring writing, understanding how genre is the key to the first page, how to write a first page for a new series, and more.

Hemingway Editor
http://hemingwayapp.com
Hemingway Editor is an editing application for those who want to self-edit their writing. Available on both a native desktop app and in-browser, Hemingway Editor goes beyond spell-checking and can help the author identify stylistic upgrades, needless words, and when your writing might be too dense. The average American reads at a tenth-grade level. Hemingway analyzes the grade level of your text in the app and will identify sentences that are hard to read. Hemingway will also offer suggestions to improve readability in potentially difficult passages.

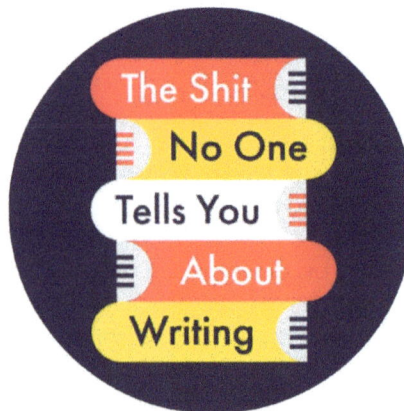

The Shit No One Tells You About Writing
https://indieauthortools.com/podcasts/the-shit-no-one-tells-you-about-writing
The Shit No One Tells You About Writing is a weekly podcast with hosts Bianca Marais, Carly Watters, and CeCe Lyra in which they interview all those involved in the publishing process, including authors, agents, and editors. Specializing in actionable discussions for emerging writers who want to improve their writing, the podcast includes a specialized segment within the show called "Books with Hooks," where hosts read and analyze query letters and the opening pages of books on air. Listeners can expect good advice and honest insight for honing their craft.

Navigating the Seas of Nautical Fiction

When delving into the world of Nautical Fiction, you might first imagine epic tales like Herman Melville's *Moby Dick* or Ernest Hemingway's *The Old Man and the Sea*. Although these classics—as well as books by Jack London, John D. McDonald, C. S. Forester, and Patrick O'Brian—undoubtedly hold a prominent place in the genre, Nautical Fiction has evolved far beyond its traditional boundaries, incorporating elements of Mystery, Fantasy, History, and Thriller stories into its narrative depths.

STEADY AS SHE GOES

Traditionally, Nautical Fiction readers have shown remarkable loyalty to series, a trend exemplified by Tripp Ellis's Tyson Wild series, which boasts an impressive sixty-seven books. According to Chris Niles, author of the Shark Key Adventure series, books in this genre typically span 70,000 to 90,000 words, with individual stories neatly contained within each installment. Rather than leaving readers on cliffhangers, these series entice readers with the question of what adventures the protagonist will embark upon next.

Although male protagonists have historically dominated Nautical Fiction, there has been a noticeable surge in the popularity of female leads in recent years. From Niles's Shark Key Adventures series, blending Contemporary Action-Adventure with historical elements, to Christine Kling's South Florida Adventure series, offering Contemporary Mystery and Suspense, and even Chloe Neill's Captain Kit Brightling series, which explores the realms of Fantasy and Young Adult fiction, female protagonists are charting new courses across the genre.

Scott W. Cook, author of numerous Nautical Fiction books such as *The Wicked Flee Where None Pursueth*, underscores the importance of the sea as a metaphor. "The sea has always been viewed as a living thing," he says, "not just because it contains so much life, but that the ocean itself is alive. So often we refer to the sea as being angry or kind. Being at sea in all weathers is such a tactile, sensory, and emotional experience that we tend to anthropomorphize it."

SHIP-SHAPE AND BRISTOL FASHION

Niles indicates her books skew to an older demographic and that other authors in the genre have reported the same. She emphasizes the importance of authenticity in Nautical Fiction, noting that readers are particularly intolerant of inaccuracies. Familiarity with nautical terms and firsthand boating, sailing, or diving experience can lend credibility to the narrative. In addition, writers should research historical contexts or geographical settings, if applicable. Visiting maritime museums, reading primary accounts, and even experiencing sailing or diving firsthand can enrich the storytelling process.

Authors exploring elements of Fantasy or Speculative Fiction within the Nautical Fiction genre should strive to strike a careful balance between realism and imagination. Fantasy oceans might differ from those in our world, such as that of Brandon Sanderson's *Tress of the Emerald Sea*, but readers should still be able to see, hear, taste, and smell that fantasy world.

For aspiring writers eager to embark on their own nautical adventures, resources abound. The Tropical Authors website (https://tropicalauthors.com) provides a wealth of information and connections within the genre, and the Nautical Writing Society Facebook Group (https://facebook.com/groups/NauticalWritingSociety) offers a platform for networking and collaboration. Additionally, writers exploring variations such as Fantasy, Thriller, Christian Fiction, or Historical narratives can find supportive communities tailored to their specific interests.

FAIR WINDS AND FOLLOWING SEAS

In the ever-expanding universe of Nautical Fiction, the horizon stretches wide, inviting writers to navigate uncharted waters and craft tales that resonate with readers while honoring the rich traditions of the genre. With dedication, authenticity, and a spirit of adventure, there's no limit to the stories waiting to be told upon the high seas of literary imagination.

KEY TROPES

- **Lone wolf solving problems authorities ignore:** The character operates independently and sometimes outside the law in order to solve a problem overlooked by the powers that be.
- **Quest:** The character embarks upon a journey toward a significant goal, facing challenges, hardships, and sacrifices along the way.
- **Search for mythical or historical artifacts or treasure:** The plot revolves around the pursuit of a significant object or legendary item of great value or power.
- **Human versus nature (specifically, the sea):** Nautical Fiction stories should center on the character's struggle against the unpredictable and often destructive forces of nature.
- **Pirates:** This can be based on historical accounts of pirates or interpretations of piracy popular in Fantasy and Sci-Fi; characters are engaged in piracy themselves or are fighting to stop pirates' endeavors. ■

Gayle Leeson

Gayle Leeson

Gayle Leeson is a USA TODAY best-selling, award-winning author who writes multiple cozy mystery series and a portal fantasy series under the pen name G. Leeson. Gayle has also written as Amanda Lee (the embroidery mystery series) and as Gayle Trent. Visit her online at gayleleeson.com.

PROSPERITY

Six Steps to Success

Many years ago, one of my mentors echoed something I'd heard from life coach Tony Robbins in my early twenties: you are cause, not effect.

Tony said it like this: the past doesn't equal the future.

I took both to mean: I am the driver, I am ultimately in control, and I can be successful at whatever I undertake. Additionally, I'm not at anyone else's mercy, and the best is yet to come.

There are a few things I wish I'd known when I was starting my writing career twenty years ago. These are the practical practices, action steps, and advice you can use, lean into, and even return to as needed as you embrace higher levels of success and prosperity in your writing career.

Sometimes you need to slow down to speed up. Before you can hit top writing speeds and gain ultimate momentum, you'll need to let go of anything that slows you down. This could include people, things, or even a tendency to procrastinate. Get organized, get focused, and then get going.

Build your protocol. Chefs practice mise en place, meaning they put everything they need, in the correct amounts, in place prior to cooking. Define what needs to be in place for you to write as your best self. Decide who you need to become to build the writing business vision you've been holding in your mind. Focus on your personal growth, and your professional growth will follow suit.

Your writing isn't an avocado. Great writing doesn't go bad; done well, the words you write can live on and bring income for many years. Take the time to produce quality work. The best news is the more you write, the more you'll write—the better your writing will get and the faster it will come. Always choose quality over quantity, and know that eventually it will lead you to produce quality quickly.

Write your next book. Every time I publish a new book, my back list sells more. I published nine books in 2023, and my backlist sales grew by over 3,000 percent. Just keep writing.

Don't half-ass it. It's much easier to talk about writing, think about writing, and wonder how you're going to earn a living from your writing than it is to actually write—until you make it your habit. There are a lot of people putting in minimal effort and expecting maximum results. Half-assing anything in your career will not cut it. Give it your all, and remember: you're going to need to use your #WholeAss.

Find people who encourage and inspire you. A mentor can compress decades of learning into days, providing a path for you to follow and helping you peek around corners with any big business decision you make (read: avoid costly time and money mistakes). A peer group of others with similar goals and visions will cheer you on and lift you up. If you want to go far, you can do it alone. But if you want to go far quickly, surround yourself with others to exponentially multiply your results—and your ultimate happiness.

One final thought: You can have, do, be, and create anything and everything you want to, and I want you to only listen to those who tell you that. Now, let's go do some writing! ∎

Honorée Corder

Honorée Corder

Honorée Corder is the author of more than fifty books, an empire builder, and encourager of writers. When she's not writing, she's spoiling her dog and two cats, eating something fabulous her husband made on the grill, working out, or reading. She hopes this article made a positive impact on your life, and if it did, you'll reach out to her via HonoreeCorder.com.

Five Tips to Free Your Mind from Analysis Paralysis

As creators, choices abound in our daily lives, from which subgenre we should write in to which software we should use to which companies we should publish with. We also make business decisions and decisions for our personal lives. And while we like to think we have unlimited mental energy, that isn't true. All those decisions take a bite out of our store of mental energy, whether small, like what clothes to wear, to larger, like deciding on a major plot direction.

A Google search for the term "analysis paralysis" gives over 58 million results, but a simple definition is the feeling of being unable to make a decision because of overthinking. Also known as decision fatigue, analysis paralysis can stem from anxiety, a fear of mistakes, imposter syndrome, or a glut of information and options. This may leave you struggling to name characters, feeling unclear on the next steps in the story, procrastinating on a preorder page, missing deadlines or opportunities, or just working much harder at basic tasks than usual.

Fortunately, there are ways to mitigate the effects of analysis paralysis.

Automate what you can. Plan out outfits, like Steve Jobs's famous repeated identical outfits; routines, such as weekly cleaning or exercise plans; or menus—create a calendar for meals that stretches a week or even a month. Automate tasks for your author business as well. You can batch-schedule social media posts or make a checklist for releases (see *IAM*'s customizable countdown checklist for a successful book launch to get started). Avoid spending your energy on simple decisions you can take off your plate.

Make important decisions when you are fresh. The time to approach those tricky decisions is when you're feeling your best. This could be first thing in the morning or after your first block of writing is done—whenever you feel well rested and recharged.

Limit input. Set limits for how much you'll allow yourself to consider a particular decision, perhaps by time or number of options. A pros and cons list can help identify what is important to you; then find a couple of options that work with those priorities and make a choice. For example, if you need to select a subscription service, the top three options that meet your needs are all you need to compare. Decide and move forward.

Stop researching once you've decided. Continuing to second-guess yourself significantly increases dissatisfaction, even if your decision is working. This can be hard to shut down, but spinning your mental wheels doesn't help your progress.

Remember that these decisions have no perfect solution. Although we long for easy, cookie-cutter concerns and clear-cut answers, life is messy. Perfection is the enemy of progress, and we all want progress!

Feelings of overwhelm and uncertainty are part of living. If you get stuck, remind yourself that it's temporary, and take a few deep breaths. Many times, taking a break, consulting a close friend, or sleeping on the problem can help. Be kind to yourself, and remember other good decisions you've made. Your decision might not be perfect, but neither are we—and a "good-enough" decision is still good. ■

Jen B. Green

Jen B. Green

Jen B. Green has lived in five countries on four continents with her three sons, two daughters, and one great guy. She reads anything that stays still long enough, plays piano, and bakes everything sweet.

After earning her Ph.D. in psychology, Jen tried writing a novel for Nanowrimo and was hooked! Her days are spent traveling the world, teaching undergraduate psychology, and wrangling her growing homemade army, but her nights are for writing Urban Fantasy with witches and werewolves.

CORNER THE MARKET

You Can Too

According to Book Report, my top-line sales income from last year was $1,724,509.13. Except it wasn't. The $1.7 million is the bulk of it, but audiobook sales, global paperback sales through Ingram-Spark, KDP All-Star bonuses, and other income streams all add to make the number roughly $2 million for 2023.

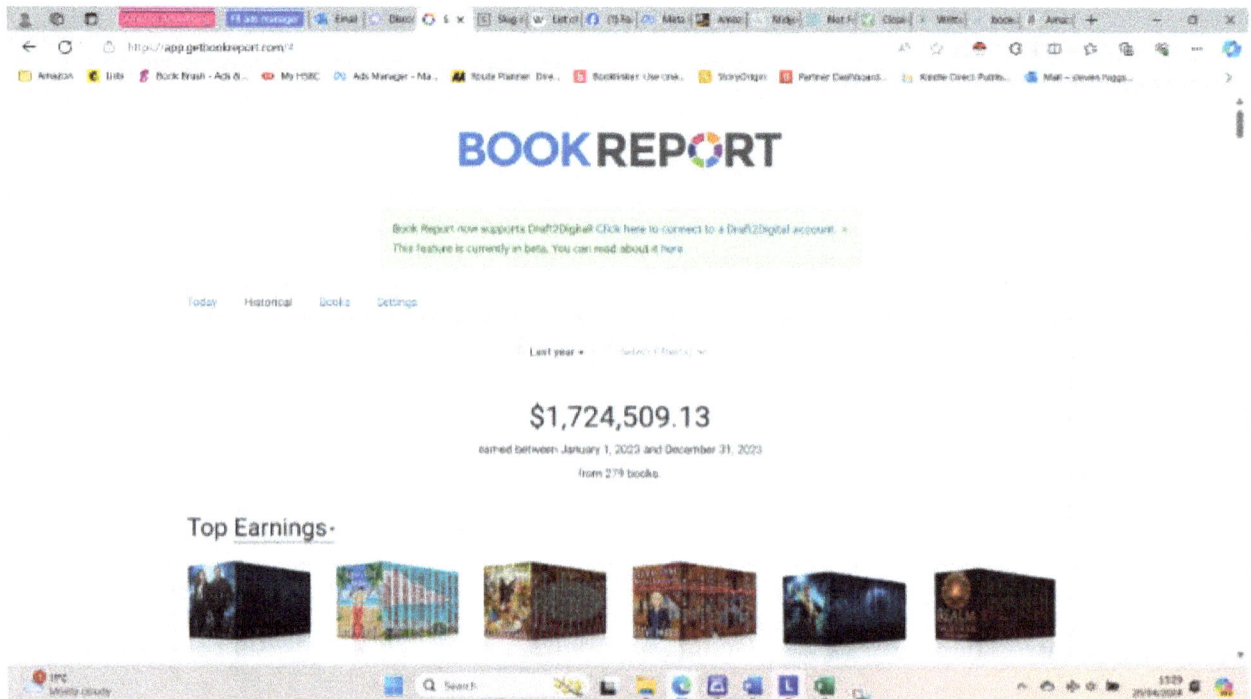

My top-line income from 2023 before adding in the earnings from other revenue streams.

Why am I showing you this? Is it because I feel a need to brag? Is my ego such that I need people to gawp at me in wonder?

No. It's because, very simply, you can do this too.

Now, you just had one of two reactions to that statement. You either leaned in because you want to see what secrets I will reveal, or you rolled your eyes and dismissed the suggestion as just plain ridiculous. I suppose there could be a third reaction where you hoped it could be true but assumed some kind of special circumstances are required for it to happen.

And that takes me nicely to the first big point: the importance of belief.

Whether you believe you can or believe you cannot, you will probably be right.

I published my first book in June 2017. It sold no copies and made no money, but I knew I could achieve a sensible income because other people were doing it. In author groups on social media, they talked about and even showed their sales figures.

It was possible, and with that in mind, I set out to be successful.

Which leads me neatly to point 2.

Your success cannot be measured by anyone other than you. For some, simply finishing the manuscript they have slaved over for years and pressing the button to publish it will be success enough. For others, the aim might be to supplant the wage from their day job. You get to decide what your goal is, and no one else should have an opinion.

What does it take?

Well, it takes hard work and probably some sacrifice. On my journey, I stopped going out, got up early to write almost every day, and went to bed late most nights after studying an element of the business. I called it "the grind" and recognized that it came from my utter determination to succeed.

If you speak to other authors making a career in this indie industry, I believe you will find their stories are much the same.

There is a lot to learn, and while many of the tasks can be outsourced, at the start of your career, you probably don't have the income to justify the outlay, and that's a good thing. You want to learn marketing, website construction, how to build your newsletter subscription list, and many more alien tasks. Only by doing so will you have the knowledge to control your subcontractors when you outsource your work.

It will take time, so allow yourself the months or years required to find your way up the mountain. It will be worth it, but never doubt your ability to get there.

Still not convinced?

Being successful as an indie author really comes down to just two things: writing books people want to read and marketing them effectively so those readers will know to make that purchase. Over time, your back list will build; every author recalls staring forlornly at the one lonely title on their KDP bookshelf. Only if you stop writing will it remain alone.

It took me five years to write my first book. Five months to write the next. I now have more than one hundred titles published, but I can name a dozen indies making more money with a fraction of that number. Some only publish a book a year.

My final point is the biggest: although I loathe to admit it, there is nothing special about me. I left school at seventeen with no education and joined the British Army. I could easily have found myself collecting shopping trolleys in a supermarket carpark. When I started to write the stories in my head, I did so with a book that taught me how to use grammar.

So believe me, if you want to be successful, if you want to make money, the pathway to do so is well trodden. All you have to do is follow where others have gone.

I wish you all the luck in the world. ■

Steve Higgs

Steve Higgs

High school Valedictorian enlists in the Marine Corps under a guaranteed tank contract. An inauspicious start that was quickly superseded by excelling in language study.

CLONE YOURSELF

Custom Chat GPT Bots

Harnessing AI's knowledge base and expand your skills and expertise in vital areas such as:

Life and Business Coaching
Mastering Marketing and Newsletter Strategies
Crafting Captivating Blurbs and Social Posts
Enhancing Time Management
Elevating Customer Service
Writing Compelling Ad, Product, and Landing Page Copy

And that's just the beginning.

INDIEAUTHORTRAINING.COM